Perspectives in Public Regulation

Essays on Political Economy

Edited with an Introduction by

MILTON RUSSELL

SOUTHERN ILLINOIS UNIVERSITY PRESS
Carbondale and Edwardsville

Feffer & Simons, Inc.
London and Amsterdam

Library of Congress Cataloging in Publication Data

Southern Illinois University Conference on Current Issues in Public
    Utility Regulation and Management, Carbondale, 1972.
    Perspectives in public regulation.

    "Sponsored by the Business Research Bureau and the Political
Economy Workshop of the Department of Economics."
    Includes bibliographical references.
    1. Public utilities--United States--Rate of return--
Congresses. 2. Public utilities--United States--Rates--
Congresses. 3. Public utilities--Social aspects--United States--
Congresses. I. Russell, Milton, 1933-   ed. II. Illinois,
Southern Illinois University, Carbondale. Business Research
Bureau. III. Illinois. Southern Illinois University, Carbondale.
Dept. of Economics. IV. Title.
hd2766.S57 1972   363.6'0973   73-9626
ISBN 0-8093-0645-X

To my parents

E. R. and Lorraine Russell

Contents

Academic Participants   ix

Preface   xiii

Notes on Contributors   xv

Introduction:
The Political Economy of Public Utilities   xix

1   Public Utilities and the Theory of Power
     Warren J. Samuels   1
     Comments by Mark V. Pauly   27

2   Practical Economics of Public Utility Regulation:
An Application to Pipelines
     Donald A. Murry   35
     Comments by Carl E. Horn   47

3   Investment Characteristics of Common Stocks in Regulated
and Unregulated Industries: A Comparative Study
     Lawrence Fisher   53
     Comments by James A. Gentry   79

4   Public Utility Regulation: Structure and Performance
     James W. McKie   85
     Comments by Stanley G. Long   104

Notes   111

Index   127

Academic Participants

RICHARD A. ARNOULD
> Assistant Professor of Economics, University of Illinois at Champaign-Urbana

JAMES L. BICKSLER
> Visiting Associate Professor of Finance, University of Illinois at Chicago Circle

RANDYL D. ELKIN
> Assistant Professor of Economics, Illinois State University

LAWRENCE FISHER
> Professor of Finance, University of Chicago

WOLF D. FUHRIG
> Professor of Political Science, MacMurray College

JAMES A. GENTRY
> Associate Professor of Finance, University of Illinois at Champaign-Urbana

PAUL GRAESER
> Assistant Professor of Economics, Northern Illinois University

PAUL E. HANCHETT
> Professor of Finance, Roosevelt University of Chicago

JAMES R. HERBSLEB
> Professor of Economics and Business Administration, Monmouth College

LAWRENCE HILL
> Assistant Professor of Economics, Lewis College

DISMAS B. KALCIC
> Associate Professor of Economics, Illinois Benedictine College

HERBERT LASKY
    Assistant Professor of History, Eastern Illinois University

CHARLES M. LINKE
    Associate Professor of Finance, University of Illinois at
    Champaign-Urbana

STANLEY G. LONG
    Associate Professor of Economics, University of Pittsburgh
    at Johnstown

DAVID C. LUAN
    Associate Professor of Economics, Southern Illinois
    University at Edwardsville

BERNARD J. MCCARNEY
    Associate Professor of Economics, Illinois State University

THOMAS F. MCMAHON
    Associate Professor of Business Law, Loyola University of
    Chicago

THOMAS D. MORGAN
    Associate Professor of Law, University of Illinois at
    Champaign-Urbana

JAMES W. MCKIE
    Dean, School of Social and Behavioral Sciences, University
    of Texas (Austin)

JOHN T. MOORE
    Professor of Marketing, Eastern Illinois University

DONALD A. MURRY
    Associate Professor of Economics, University of Missouri-St.
    Louis

JAMES F. NISS
    Associate Professor of Economics, Western Illinois University

MARK V. PAULY
    Associate Professor of Economics, Northwestern University

HOWARD G. ROEPKE
    Professor of Geography, University of Illinois at Champaign-
    Urbana

MILTON RUSSELL
    Professor of Economics, Southern Illinois University at
    Carbondale

WARREN J. SAMUELS
    Professor of Economics, Michigan State University

DANIEL D. SINGER
    Assistant Professor of Economics, Western Illinois University

MICHAEL A. STOLLER
    Assistant Professor of Economics, Millikin University

LESLIE SZEPLAKI
    Assistant Professor of Economics, Loyola University of
    Chicago

DAVID B. VELLENGA
    Assistant Professor of Management, University of Illinois
    at Chicago Circle

BISMARCK WILLIAMS
    Professor of Finance, Roosevelt University of Chicago

Preface

The essays and comments in this volume are revisions of those
originally presented at the Southern Illinois University Conference on Current Issues in Public Utility Regulation and Management
held September 1972. Sponsored by the Business Research Bureau and
the Political Economy Workshop of the Department of Economics,
this conference was made possible by financial support from
Illinois Bell Telephone Company. The contributions here are the
sole responsibility of the authors and do not necessarily represent the views of any of the sponsoring organizations.

An important contribution to the success of the conference,
and of this volume, was made by the conference participants. This
group included academics from such diverse disciplines as economics, political science, finance, law, and history, and an invited
group of Illinois Bell executives. Revisions of the essays and
comments for publication took into account many of the views expressed by these participants.

The premise underlying this conference was that research
bearing on the regulated industries has undergone a striking
transformation in the last decade or so. The established empirical
and institutional approach has been augmented and supported by an
infusion of modern theoretical and political analysis. In con-
junction with this transformation, there has been a resurgence of
interest in the operation and control of these fundamental industries. Observers have begun to realize that utilities are not the
stable, dull purveyors of standardized services they were once
thought to be. Rapid growth, technological change, competitive
market penetration, environmental effects, social responsibility--
these are among the stimuli for research that have caught the
imagination of academicians, students, and businessmen alike.

By the variety of its methodology and subject matter, the
research reported here should demonstrate the breadth of scholar-
ship that has been focused on regulatory problems. Hopefully, it
should also illuminate opportunities for further scholarly research.

Anne Newcombe of the Business Research Bureau staff assisted
with the administrative arrangements for the conference and with
the editing of the essays. Pam Schilling typed the manuscript.
The clerical work and facilities were provided by the Business
Research Bureau, Allan Pulsipher, director. The editor assumed
total control and direction of the organization of the conference,
the selection of participants, the selection of contributors, dis-
cussants, and topics, and the decisions involved in the final

preparation of this volume. All errors of omission and commission
are therefore his responsibility alone.

                                                              Milton Russell

Carbondale, Illinois
January 1973

Notes on Contributors

LAWRENCE FISHER is Professor of Finance, Graduate School of Business, University of Chicago, and Associate Director of the School's Center for Research in Security Prices (sponsored by Merrill Lynch, Pierce, Fenner & Smith, Inc.). In the latter capacity, he has been involved since 1960 in the Center's development of a data bank of New York Stock Exchange market transactions. In addition to his work with the Center, Dr. Fisher has served as consultant to numerous organizations, including Standard and Poor's; the Chicago Board of Trade; AT&T; Merrill Lynch, Pierce, Fenner & Smith, Inc.; and RAND. His scholarly articles have appeared in such journals as the Journal of Political Economy, the Journal of Business, the Financial Analysts Journal, and the International Economic Review.

JAMES A GENTRY is Associate Professor of Finance at the University of Illinois. He previously taught at Indiana University, where he received his M.B.A. and D.B.A. degrees. Before entering teaching, Dr. Gentry was an account executive with Dean Witter and Company in Fresno, California. He has published numerous articles in business and finance journals, most recently "Rates of Return on Common Stock Portfolios of Life Insurance Companies: Addendum," Journal of Risk Insurance, June 1971.

CARL E. HORN is Assistant Vice President for Planning, Illinois Bell Telephone Company. He has been associated with the Bell System since 1960 in Baltimore, New York, and Chicago in such diverse departments as traffic, marketing, public relations, accounting, revenue requirements, and planning. A graduate of Northwestern University, Mr. Horn received an M.B.A. and an M.A. in political science from the University of Chicago.

STANLEY G. LONG is Associate Professor of Economics at the University of Pittsburgh at Johnstown. He previously taught at Iowa State University, Lawrence College, and Knox College. Dr. Long received his Ph.D. degree from the University of Iowa. His current research interests include environmental economics and medical economics.

JAMES W. MCKIE is Dean, School of Social and Behavioral Sciences, University of Texas (Austin). Dean McKie's distinguished career has affected most of the exciting issues in public

regulation during the last two decades. He has been a consultant to RAND, the Council of Economic Advisors, the Antitrust
Division of the Department of Justice, and the Office of Emer-
gency Preparedness. He was a member of the White House Task
Force on Oil Imports Control. He has been a Senior Fellow at
the Brookings Institution and a member of the Brookings Advisory Committee for Studies of Regulation of Economic Activity.
Past president of the Southern Economic Association, he has
also served as editor of its journal. His articles have
appeared in the American Economic Review, the Quarterly
Journal of Economics, the Southern Economic Journal, and in
numerous collected volumes. His most recent works are "Fuel
Prices and the Regulatory Agencies," in Reforming Regulation,
ed. Roger E. Noll (1971), and "Organization and Efficiency,"
Southern Economic Journal, April 1972.

DONALD A. MURRY is Associate Dean of Faculties and Associate Professor of Economics at the University of Missouri-St. Louis.
In 1971-72, he was Chief, Division of Economic Studies of the
Federal Power Commission. He has been a consultant on regulatory matters to the Federal Power Commission, the Missouri
Public Service Commission, the County of St. Louis, the City
of Chicago, the Attorney General of Illinois, and numerous
other agencies and corporations. He has testified before the
Federal Power Commission, the Interstate Commerce Commission,
the Illinois Commerce Commission, and the Missouri Public Service Commission. His publications have been primarily in the
areas of public utility regulation and research administration.

MARK V. PAULY is Associate Professor of Economics at Northwestern
University. He is the author of Medical Care at Public Expense
(1971), as well as of numerous articles in scholarly journals,
most recently (with Richard Kilhstrom) "Role of Insurance in
the Allocation of Risk," American Economic Review, May 1971,
and "Optimality, 'Public' Goods, and Local Governments: A
General Theoretical Analysis," Journal of Political Economy,
May-June 1970. Dr. Pauly received his M.A. degree from the
University of Delaware and his Ph.D. degree from the University of Virginia.

MILTON RUSSELL is Professor of Economics, Southern Illinois University at Carbondale. Dr. Russell has focused on the economics of natural gas regulation as his special interest within
the regulatory sector. While on leave from Southern Illinois
University, he served one year in the Office of Economics,
Federal Power Commission, and has been a consultant for both
the Federal Power Commission and Resources for the Future on
regulatory matters. Among his publications in the regulatory
field are the recent book (with Laurence A. Toenjes) Natural
Gas Producer Regulation and Taxation (1972); "Producer Regulation for the 1970's" in Regulation of the Natural Gas
Producing Industry, ed. Keith Brown (1972); and "Resource

Allocation and Utility Certification Decisions" in Manley
Irwin and Milton Russell, Selected Structure and Allocation
Problems in the Regulated Industries (1969).

WARREN J. SAMUELS is Professor of Economics at Michigan State Uni-
versity and is the editor of the Journal of Economic Issues.
Dr. Samuels's essay is the outgrowth of a career-long interest
in the boundary areas joining political and economic phenomena.
Two of his recent contributions to this study are his articles,
"Externalities, Rate Structure and the Theory of Public Utility Regulation," in Essays on Public Utility Pricing and
Regulation, ed. Harry M. Trebing, and "Interrelations Between
Legal and Economic Processes," Journal of Law and Economics,
October 1971. He has published extensively on regulatory and
other topics in the Public Utilities Fortnightly, Land Economics, Journal of Economic Issues, Southern Economic Journal,
and Quarterly Journal of Economics.

Introduction
The Political Economy of Public Utilities

Public utility enterprises, as variously defined, have received
differential treatment by public authorities almost since the
beginning of organized government. Looking back through the cen-
turies, postures of government regarding public utilities can
be found along a spectrum from nurture and protection to repres-
sion. Much recent revisionist study of the American experience
has suggested that in origin, intent, and action regulatory agencies can best be understood as fulfilling the goals of the regulated,
or of a sub-set of them. Nonetheless, the mainstream rationale
for special government attention to certain industries has been to
enhance the general interest of the public, as contrasted to the
special interest of the regulated. Even within this tradition,
however, three distinct emphases can be identified in just the
twentieth century. At the risk of oversimplification, these
emphases may be denoted as the restriction of monopoly profits,
improved resource allocation, and political economy. These phases
are neither temporally discrete nor are practitioners nicely
identified with each, but the categories themselves are useful
in understanding differences and conflicts in views of regulatory
decision-making. The comments below are addressed to these approaches to the evaluation of regulatory decision-making, ac-
cepting for this argument the validity of the ostensible general
interest motivation for public regulation.

The "old-line" regulation to limit monopoly profits grew out
of the populist spirit that monopoly was evil in and of itself,
but especially so when it led to redistribution of income toward
the powerful (owners) and away from the weak (consumers). This
spirit of almost vindictive control of public utilities reached
its zenith during the 1930s, when along with a reformist era and
a disillusionment with business enterprise, the results of in-
vestigations into corporate wrongdoing were widely disseminated.
Regulation took on the aura of a holy war in which the protagonists
were good and evil, and one needed no scorecard to tell which was
which.

The focus of regulation in this spirit was on the direct redistribution of income from the regulated firm to its consumers.
The decision variable was recorded rate of return on rate base,
not particular rates themselves. The rarely, (if ever) tested, but
implicit, assumptions were that lower rates of return caused income to be redistributed toward consumers, and income redistributed
toward consumers was transferred downward in the income scale.
These propositions, while intuitively reasonable, are not obvious

in an era of pension fund and foundation investment in utility
stocks, of income taxes, of uncertain income elasticity of demand
for utility services, of extraordinary utility capital needs to
meet demand expansion, and of uncertain regulatory effects on the
efficiency of resource allocation. When coupled with unsupervised
utility control of rate structures and service quality, restriction
on profit levels alone may have perverse effects on income distribution. Limitation of economic rents and monopoly profits, moreover, is static in outlook and, like the law, backward looking in
perspective. There is no necessary connection between lower rates
of return and lower long-term rates for services. Further, he who
wishes only to limit monopoly profits must first measure them,
which means that it is to what has happened, not what might be
that regulatory attention is directed. Alternatives foregone are
never considered, and potential rewards to consumers through incentives to different patterns of operation are never within the
decision matrix.

Regulation focused on rate of return on rate base is negative
in its essence and direct in its approach. The sanction of rate
reductions or of limiting rate increases is not balanced, except
fortuitously, by incentives toward efficiency, improved performance, or innovative development. Positive disincentives, in
fact, are created by the punitive approach toward the successful
risky venture. In sum, it can be argued that exclusive use of the
return on rate base instrument of regulation is flawed because it
does not necessarily fulfill even its limited objective of res-
stricting monopoly profits, and it certainly may not fulfill the
rationale for this objective, the improvement of the absolute and
relative well being of relatively lower income consumers.

Despite the limitations considered above, emphasis on the restriction of the rate of monopoly profits has fulfilled some well
articulated social goals, and though criticized, has remained
politically viable. Perhaps most important to its continuing
vitality is that rate of return regulation is entrenched in the
legal processes and embodied in statute. Even critics and doubters
of this mode know that its legal outcome is predictable, whatever
the economic or social implications of regulation motivated and
posited on the atomistic case by case approach. Observed monopoly return is limited, as is politically sensitive economic
power, and opportunity for gross and obvious exploitation of consumers is reduced. The more settled the technology, the more
stable the environment, the more secure the market, and the less
significant the opportunities to do better what is done acceptably,
the more satisfactory is public utility regulation in this traditional mold.

The full policy implications of rate of return regulation only
became visible with the development of welfare economics, using
econometric estimation techniques and systemic analysis. Regulators alerted to these developments shifted their attention away
from the regulated firm and toward consumers and the broader public. Along with most modern economists, these analysts adopted
the efficiency criterion as their policy guide, explicitly avoiding

efforts to shift income. The normative goal became maximization of
economic welfare, which, when joined with the behavioral postulate
of individual pecuniary maximization, provided a predictive theory
as well. Income distribution concerns were identified, of course,
but were explicitly reserved for attention through other instruments, most usually government tax and expenditure actions. Con-
currently, the actual income distribution effects of regulation
were subjected to estimation, with results that sometimes cast
doubt on the efficiency of existing regulatory procedures in fulfilling their presumed goals.

Three matters have attracted the attention of regulatory analysts following this welfare economics path. These have been first,
the effects of existing forms of regulation on the efficiency of
utility performance; second, the effect of rate structures on
resource allocation; and finally, the direct and indirect costs of
regulation. Policy recommendations of deregulation or of regulation on some other standard have often followed from these inves-
tigations. Such recommendations were predicated, of course, on
the normative value of welfare maximization (as defined).

Rate of return on rate base regulation has, according to this
analysis, failed because it has not minimized the social costs of
the benefits flowing to the public from the regulated industries.
The willingness of utilities to undertake somewhat risky but
socially remunerative ventures has been reduced. Other incentives
have been generated which lead to the inflation of the cost of
service. The propensity to shift profits to management and stockholders by unnecessary or excessive spending on amenities has been
identified. Nonoptimal production functions, as per the Averch-
Johnson hypothesis, have been shown to be consistent with maximum
utility profits under regulatory constraints. Excessive timidity
for fear of public response (the choice of the "quiet life") and
supraoptimal quality performance standards also have been charged
to the established regulatory process. More significant still,
economists have noted that regulatory restraint plus the market
security of regulatory status would tend to dampen incentives for
optimal development over time. While formidable, these criticisms
have not been dispositive. By the nature of the case, most of
these effects cannot be tested empirically. The effect of recognizing the incompleteness of the characterization of human behavior
and of the public interest which underlies these conclusions will
be addressed later.

Rate design (the pattern of particular rates for different
utility services) has been another of the major operational concerns of the modern welfare economists who have addressed regulatory matters. Adherence to the principle, if not the immutable
practice, of marginal cost pricing is the litmus test for adherence to the welfare approach to regulation. The regulatory agencies
and the regulated firms have been exposed to innumerable schemes
for moving closer to marginal costing principles. Estimates of
welfare benefits from such schemes have been made. The failures
of preexisting regulation when measured by the marginal cost pricing standard have been identified. While welfare theorists have

reminded one another of the problems of the "second best" and of
the impossibility of nondistorting taxes and subsidies, these are
not the arguments which have limited marginal cost pricing in
practice. In operation, marginal cost pricing has been limited
because of its effects on monopoly profits, income distribution,
and on the achievement of other social goals. Within the delimited
welfare model such matters are either ignored or rationalized, but
not in the world in which the regulated, the regulatory agencies,
and the public live.

The cost of regulation must be compared with its benefits at
the margin before optimal decisions can be made if one's concern
is with welfare maximizing policy. In this framework the benefits
from alterations in the distribution of income are merely the
social gain from that distributional change, impossible to measure
but almost certainly lower than the total amount of income redistributed. Resource gains (benefits) can also arise from improvements in allocation brought on by regulation, especially from the
effect of moving closer to the (presumed) optimal output where
price is equal to marginal cost. On the other hand, the direct
costs of regulation on the part of all interests reduce the resources available to satisfy other wants. Moreover, regulatory
actions can distort economic decisions leading to sometimes significant resource misallocations and to sharp reductions in the
value of total output. Through the use of econometric techniques
such losses in welfare may be estimated.

Selection of the policy standards of modern welfare economics
represents as distorted a view of the public's interest in utility
regulation as would acceptance of the populist attitude that restriction of monopoly profit is an indication of regulatory
success. The failure of welfare economics to alter significantly
the course of regulation is not due to a failure of logic or analysis but instead to a failure to specify goals correctly and to
a failure to assimilate into its policy recommendations the complexity of human motivation. As a result, its predictions fail and
its policy recommendations are ignored. Certainly, welfare economics provides a measure of some of the costs and benefits of
regulation. Further, welfare economics demonstrates the emptiness
of redistribution per se as the economic goal. It is indeed important for policy makers to know that regulatory intervention
may create the anti-Paretian effect of making many worse off without making anyone better off. Welfare economics has contributed
to improved regulation by almost any value standard. The public
has not, however, accepted its normative criterion for judging
policy, nor have predictions of policy or of behavior relying on
the welfare model been satisfactory. To rely on welfare economics
alone is to condemn the analyst to impotence in the face of the
complexity of the regulatory process.

While social behavior has never been simple, analysts have
ever been searching for unifying simple theories to predict it
and, as importantly for our purposes, for simple and universal
rules by which we could judge the wisdom and efficiency of particular policies. We have seen that there is disagreement among

public utility analysts about the nature of human behavior and
thus about the goals for public policy. A simple vision of the
role of regulation has arisen consistent with two such positions:
on the one hand there is regulation as a limiter of monopoly profits and, on the other, there is regulation as a promoter of the
"optimal" allocation of resources. Neither view has achieved universality and thus been accepted as a normative standard, and
each has failed the predictive test, as the actual course of policy shows. Three examples of the recent use of the public utility
institution to ameliorate social problems illustrate the predictive bankruptcy and normative failure of both the simple constructs
we have posited here.

The Federal Power Commission during the 1960s, without fan-
fare or much public attention, began requiring in its certification
orders that all waterpower sites be open to public recreation and
other use on a nondiscriminatory basis, and that public notice
to that effect be posted. Yet, oversight of the race, sex, creed,
or ethnic origin of water skiers in lakes formed by power dams
is not required to assure the provision of adequate utility service at fair and reasonable rates. The level of monopoly profits
is not likely to be affected. A case might be made that free
public access to recreation is necessary for maximum economic
welfare, but such an argument could not be based on, or limited
to facilities enjoying, public utility status. The FPC inserted
this requirement because to do so seemed to the commissioners to
be consistent with the national interest in fostering a harmonious
multiracial society. Restricting monopoly profits or improving
resource allocation had nothing to do with it.

Utility regulation qua utility regulation has introduced environmental protection into regulatory proceedings by requiring
certain behavior and allowing its cost to be covered by consumer
rates. While optimal resource allocation would require the in-
ternalization of all externalities, no argument can be made for
special treatment of public utilities on economic or statutory
grounds. It can even be shown that total environmental quality
might be reduced if extraordinary pressures were placed on utilities to limit their emissions. At the same time, required environmental protection efforts have not been formulated and enforced
to lower monopoly profits. Public utilities, however, have been
among the prime targets of all of those seeking to restrict harm-
ful emissions, and regulation has accommodated these pressures.
As just one indication of the level of this involvement, 50 percent or more of the major articles in the Public Utilities Fortnightly during 1972 have, in lesser or greater degree, concerned
environmental quality or other externality issues. If neither
welfare economics nor the restriction of monopoly profits can explain this development, some other approach is required.

As a final example, public utilities have been exposed to
intense pressures to rectify generations of educational and social
neglect (and overt discrimination) by active policies of recruit-
ment and promotion of members of minority groups. It is understand-
able that because of lack of visibility small firms would be less

subjected to pressure by affirmative action agencies than would be large enterprises. There is no reason grounded in the economics of optimal resource allocation, the goal of restricting monopoly exactions, or the usual regulatory statutes to explain why public utilities should be singled out. They are, however, and a coherent approach to the public utility institution should be able to explain why.

In each of these situations, then, public utilities as public utilities are required to act to foster social goals not peculiarly associated with their economic function of producing specified services for specified markets. Service costs are increased, and such costs (or most of them) are passed on to consumers. The effect is to use the regulatory instrument to transfer income (monetary and/or imputed) away from rate payers and, to a lesser degree, away from managers and stockholders. Income is transferred to those who particularly value environmental quality, those who belong to minority groups and those to whom the satisfaction of these goals for others bears particular value. These transfers are not directly consistent with either the rationale of restriction of monopoly profit or with the rationale of optimal allocation of resources. Sole reliance on either of these constructs would leave the analyst little of substance to say about some of the most pervasive issues in public utility regulation. These approaches thus fail as bases of predicting what will occur in regulatory proceedings, and they fail as well in specifying the values which are dominant in the economy. At best then, they exist as expressions of some elements of the total set of norms which guide policy formulation and then sanction its results.

The questions remain, why has economic reasoning not been dispositive in regulatory proceedings? And second, how might economists become more useful as analysts of the regulatory process? The appropriate response, I would suggest, involves the identification of three matters. First, economists have failed to recognize the multiplicity of goals. Second, they have consistently misjudged or misunderstood what policy goals are. Finally, economists have developed and used tools which can only deal with the goal or goals they perceive, rather than with the multiplicity of goals which actually exist and among which policy must achieve an accommodation.

For the most part economists of all stripes have perceived goals in terms of proximate economic results and have ignored the effects on other goals of the process by which those results are reached. To illustrate: the economists who as social critics wanted to make consumers relatively better off perhaps started with the proximate policy goals of minimizing monopoly profits. Yet it is axiomatic that it is possible to reduce monopoly profits by a process which leaves consumers worse off than they might be even with no regulation whatsoever. The difficulties of maintaining technological progress, generating performance incentives, maximizing resource use efficiency, avoiding misappropriation of funds, and avoiding capital wastage are well known to any practitioner who has observed the results of restricted return-on-rate

base regulation. To look only at the results of economic activity
for the firm, without taking account of the effect on the broader
public, is a clear example of misspecifying the policy goals. Moreover, there is no reason to presume that the goal of improving the
relative position of consumers was in fact shared by the regulators themselves.

An exactly analogous case may be made with reference to the
analysts who concentrate on welfare maximization as the single
policy goal. Marginal cost pricing, the direct flow-through of
allocable cost, the avoidance of misallocation brought on by excessive service requirements, and immediate entry when technology
permits competitive provision of services are all prescriptions
consistent with the goal of maximum economic welfare. Each has
been rejected in the hurly-burly of regulatory decision-making.
Maximizing economic welfare, like minimizing monopoly profits, is
a possible goal, but not one lexicographically superior to others.
To seek to achieve it without recognizing the effect of the process of doing so leads to a policy in conflict with other strongly
held social values. The insistence on the priority of allocational
goals has condemned economists to near irrelevance and uselessness
in the policy process. Because of the obduracy of economists, the
analysis of allocational effects has often been neglected where it
could have been of greatest assistance, that is, in establishing
some ordering between two otherwise socially acceptable policies.

The conference from which these essays were drawn was designed
to approach the problems of public utility management and regulation from a somewhat different point of view. A short description
of this approach, labeled here political economy, would recognize
that it accepts the diversity and sometimes inconsistency of the
goals that simultaneously motivate human behavior. Having done so,
it examines the interaction of those goals with available instruments to generate policy. Its normative role would feature the
evaluation of policy results in terms of social goals, with the
end in view of adjusting policy instruments should inconsistency
be present. On the operational level, then, the political economy
approach would predict the use of existing or already legitimized
institutions to achieve results which are optimal partly because
they are consistent with an ongoing process, and not wholly in the
sense that they maximize some predetermined variable.

The use of the historic term political economy to designate
this approach distorts but little the term's ancient and honorable
meaning. The issues and processes dealt with here are similar to
those which mobilized the earliest classical economists, and their
view of the world as a holistic system remains. Despite the simi-
larities, however, vital differences exist: modern political economy starts with the presumption that institutions are resistant
to change but mutable, human goals are multifaceted, and that government is an available, useful, though like all other institutions, flawed instrument of social policy.

The essays in this volume were commissioned to explore aspects
of public utility management and regulation which would, taken
together, provide some perspective on the public utility

institution. The nuts and bolts of regulation were avoided in
order to devote more space to the issue of the ability of regulated firms both constrained and reinforced by public bodies to
satisfy diverse social goals. These goals are at least a more
equal distribution of income and status, efficient resource allocation, alteration or legitimization of the distribution of power,
consumer satisfaction, perceived procedural legitimacy, technological progress and economic growth.

Warren J. Samuels's essay explores the acquisition and distribution of power as an organizing principle in understanding the
behavior of both regulated firms and regulatory agencies. He suggests that both the legal and the economic paradigms are incomplete
and oversimplified. They do not predict much of the observed
action of utilities and their regulators, and they do not explain
the development of the institutions which now exist. He concludes
that the power paradigm he proposes is both more comprehensive and
dynamic. It subsumes the issues of property rights, income distribution, and resource allocation, and in addition provides a framework for analyzing and predicting behavioral response to the presence of power. In sum, Samuels's essay opens new possibilities
for a general theory of public utility behavior. Mark V. Pauly's
discussion points up Samuels's failure as yet to achieve an operational theory. He proffers some suggestions as to what such a
theory requires before it may be formulated and tested.

In a very different vein, and from a different perspective,
Donald A. Murry examines the usefulness in regulatory procedures
of some conclusions drawn from the Averch-Johnson-Wellisz model.
By structuring the problem he demonstrates the ambivalent position
of the conscientious regulator. On the one hand, efficient resource
allocation can generate levels of economic rent considered abhor-
rent to widely held standards of equity. Yet, suboptimal resource
allocation and consequent economic waste could accompany regulation consistent with equity standards. A coherent rationale does
not exist to balance the interests at stake or to formulate a
generally satisfactory solution. A regulatory solution will arise,
but not a simple one, nor one predicted by the formal model nor
one consistent with maximizing any one variable. His essay, then,
stands as an illustration of the need for rational thought as to
how goal conflicts may be resolved. His example posits forcefully
the proposition that even in a reasonably straightforward matter,
there are formidable difficulties in making economic theory operational in the regulatory context. Carl Horn, in his response to
Murry, is in essential agreement with the proposition that results
of regulatory proceedings can neither be understood nor predicted
by use of simple economic models of regulatory behavior.

One of the absorbing issues in public utility regulation and
management is whether, despite all of the effort involved on both
sides, regulation makes any difference in the outcome of economic
processes. Some of the analysts of regulation hold that because
of a congerie of circumstances, regulation in fact has no effect
on the distribution of income, the actual rate of utility return,
or on the risk of utility investment. Because of the realities of

power, it is held, monopolists get their way, protected from public scrutiny by a mere facade of regulation. Still another position is that regulated firms are so constrained by competitive market forces that regulation itself has no effect--no excessive profits would accrue anyway. Other observers have maintained that regulation was effective, but primarily in altering the allocation of resources away from the optimal, not in redistributing income. Some hold that preregulation market structure determines whether regulation has an effect, and also determines whether that effect, if it exists, will support or restrict utility satisfactions. To move these disagreements from the realm of supposition and special pleading, it is first necessary to determine whether regulated status brought any changes in financial results to regulated firms, and then to determine whether those changes were in the direction expected. Lawrence Fisher approaches this issue through the medium of the price behavior of regulated utility securities. He tests the hypotheses on regulatory effect by using the uniquely comprehensive file of data from the Center for Research in Security Prices. Fisher, and the discussant of his essay, James A. Gentry, present conclusions basic to the future development and evaluation of regulatory policy.

The final essay in this volume posits the crucial question at the heart of the political economy of regulation: How can performance be judged or policy formulated when technological change alters the effect of the institutions which previously produced viable results? James W. McKie's essay combines a sensitivity to the public interest in equity with a careful articulation of the economic costs of the dynamic misallocation of resources. He focuses on the institutional structure within which decisions are made and demonstrates the way technological change, by making competitive entry possible, can disrupt the established order. Stanley G. Long, commenting on McKie's conclusions, starts with the assumption that policy exists to maximize welfare. He concludes that it does this best by avoiding intervention in the market unless faced with a clear and present opportunity to improve allocation. By this light much of the regulatory apparatus has left the economy worse off, or at the very least, the matter of improvement is an open question.

These last contributions bring us back to the central theme of this book, what perspective can we gain on public utility regulation and management? Our conclusions are partial and somewhat unsatisfying. First, regulation as more or less traditionally practiced is a pervasive element in our economy, it is politically popular, and if a prediction were required, its ambit is more likely to expand than to contract. Second, neither of the two usual economic subparadigms are particularly useful in analyzing the regulation that exists or in predicting changes in it. We can rest no solid predictions about actual behavior on either the efficient allocation or the profit restriction hypotheses of regulatory goals. Third, to understand regulation it appears that we should seek laws governing the process of institutional decision making, not functions predicated on maximizing a single formulated

and strictly articulated goal. Fourth, values and goals differ
among men of good will and integrity, as do perceptions of reality.
Motives for actions can be misinterpreted dramatically when goals
and perceptions differ. Finally, in the adversary positions and
posturings of conflicting parties, one goal alone lays claim to
near universality. That goal is maintaining the continuity of the
process of regulation itself.

PERSPECTIVES IN PUBLIC REGULATION

1

Public Utilities and the Theory of Power

Warren J. Samuels

Public life with its complex and contradictory demands
on his loyalties, is morally confusing to the ordinary
man.--Louis L. Jaffe, "The Effective Limits of the Administrative Process: A Reevaluation"

There are as many critics of regulation as there are
interests to be served. . . . The defendant regulator
suffers the disadvantage of having to demonstrate some
central thread of consistency among the myriad of choices
facing him. His critics are free to grind a single-bitted
axe. The regulator knows that he cannot give full weight
to each and every one of the contesting elements. The
critic could care less.--John A. Carver, in A Critique
of Administrative Regulation of Public Utilities, ed.
Harry M. Trebing and Warren J. Samuels

Rather than a single social welfare function there are
many, each expressing the evaluations of different groups
of people. Which one is chosen for the purpose of solv-
ing the problem of allocation depends upon the institutional framework within which society decides upon such
matters.--James M. Henderson and Richard E. Quandt,
Microeconomic Theory

The purpose of this essay is to present an interpretation of the
public utility institution in terms of a theory of power. The
essay will present a model or paradigm of power and characterize
the public utility institution in its terms. It will show how the
public utility institution illustrates the basic model and principles of the theory of power presented, and also will interpret
and place in perspective certain important phenomena and problems
of the institution.
   The public utility institution has been understood primarily
in terms of the legal paradigm concentrating upon the indentifica-
tion and protection of rights of substance and procedure and the
economic paradigm concentrating upon the efficient allocation of
resources through market exchange. These paradigms represent

1

incomplete, partial interdependence type problem approaches which
have never been fully or satisfactorily integrated with each other:
while the legal paradigm has generally neglected efficiency, or
handled it directly, the economic paradigm takes for granted the
identification and assignment of rights in terms of which efficiency in the sense of Pareto-optimality has to be specified.[1]
Euqally important, both of these paradigms are for the most part
normative, and have been used to ground rationalizing defenses and
criticisms of the institution or elements or facets thereof.[2]

This essay offers a third and radically different paradigm.
First, the paradigm is in terms of power; second, it attempts relative comprehensiveness as a general interdependence paradigm; and
third, it attempts morally neutral, positive description of the
institution which cannot properly be used either to defend or
criticize without an additional normative premise. In each of
these respects, the essay will involve a substantial shift in the
type of thinking or analysis being undertaken.

The essay has several limitations of which I shall specify
only three. First, it is more an outline than a complete statement
and is often cryptic in its treatment of fundamental problems.
Although I have tried throughout to state my points as baldly as
possible, a bald statement produces incompleteness inasmuch as all
points have subtle nuances and complications that are omitted.

Second, I abstract from the heterogeneous legal-economic positions and roles of the several regulatory commissions. There are
significant differences among commissions, both between state and
federal levels and on each level, but the analysis is intended to
apply to all of them generally and, unfortunately, indiscriminately.

Third, the concept and language of "power" is difficult for
some to work with. Power can be seen as demeaning and sordid.
Moreover, different persons have different perceptions as to when
power is involved and when not. But it is the premise and argument
of the essay that power in a neutral, nonpejorative, and descriptive sense is the essence of the public utility institution and of
most, if not all, related problems.

The procedure will be as follows. In section 2, aspects of the
general model and principles of the theory of power are outlined.
In section 3, the public utility institution is interpreted in the
context of the model and principles. Both the model of power and
interpretation of the public utility institution are stated in
terms of general interdependence, and since analysis cannot deal
with all relevant aspects simultaneously, I acknowledge both the
arbitrary element in determining when certain interpretive points
are introduced and some unfortunately necessary redundancy. The
quasi-outline form should emphasize the paradigm-level character
of the analysis.

2. THE THEORY OF POWER

2.A. A General Paradigm of Choice and Power

A.1. The total society, the economy, and institutions are decision-making, or choice, or power, structures and processes.[3] The economy and particular institutions or clusters of institutions are decision-making subsystems of the total social decision-making system. Effective choices made by or through a decision-making process constitute its policy.

A.2. Given the general conditions of scarcity and interdependence, collective or social choice involves the disaggregation of scarcity and decision-making among the actors comprising the particular decision-making process in question. A number of definitions will be helpful here.

2.a. Opportunity set: available alternative lines of action or choices, each with a relative opportunity cost. Abstractly considered, society has a grand opportunity set which is disaggregated into the structure of opportunity sets as between individuals and institutions and other subgroups. Effective social choice from within the aggregate social opportunity set results from the aggregate interaction of individuals, institutions and other subgroups making choices from within their relevant opportunity sets.

2.b. Power: (a) effective participation in decision making; (b) the means or capacity with which to exercise choice, to participate in decision making, e.g., property, position, rights in general. The former requires the latter, and the latter makes the former possible (subject to the operation of the principles of power discussed below). Power is used here primarily with the second connotation, but usually to the effect of the first.

2.c. Coercion (constraint): impact of the behavior and choices of others upon the structure of one's opportunity set; assuming general interdependence and possession of power by all groups to some degree, this impact is mutual or reciprocal, producing a system of mutual coercion or mutual constraint. The system includes both injuries and benefits visited through action or choices of others (externalities may be defined as the substance of mutual coercion).

2.d. Working rules: rules of law and morality, etc., governing access to and use of power.

A.3. Each individual, institution or subgroup has an opportunity set of alternatives depending upon its power and the process of mutual coercion. Mutual coercion exists through the making of choices (decisions, policies) which have an effect on others' opportunity sets or power positions.

A.4. The scope of policy includes (a) the subject-matter with respect to which the individual, institution, or subgroup makes decisions and (b) the structure of the decision-making process itself (including the structure of opportunity sets). The group involved in decision-making may be different from (e.g., smaller than) the group affected by the decisions.

A.5.   All institutions function to structure the distribution
of power and are objects of capture and instruments of power
players. The operation of institutions depends upon the uses to
which the institutions are put by those who gain control and whose
interest and/or ends the institutions come to represent.

A.6.   Society has a number of social control systems or institutions which function, <u>inter alia</u>, to control the allocation of
power, resolve conflict, and integrate individuals into society,
e.g., law (state, government), custom, morality, religion, education, corporation, market. These social control systems or institutions, or those who act in the name of or in control of them,
tend to act as power players.

A.7.   The total social decision-making process and subprocesses thereof constitute a dynamic general interdependence or
general equilibrium system. Whereas most social science models are
partial interdependence (with regard to the scope of variables included and/or lines of postulated or studied causation), the model
developed here is indicated by several representative sets of dual
relationships:

(a)   the working rules of law and morals govern the dis-
      tribution and exercise of power <u>and</u> the distribution
      and exercise of power govern the development of the
      working rules;

(b)   values depend upon the decision-making process <u>and</u>
      the decision-making process depends upon values;

(c)   tastes and preferences depend upon the institutional
      structure <u>and</u> the institutional structure depends
      upon tastes and preferences;

(d)   The opportunity set of an individual depends upon the
      total structure of power <u>and</u> the total structure of
      power depends upon the decisions made by individuals
      from within their opportunity sets at any point in
      time and over time;

(e)   the power structure is a function of power play <u>and</u>
      power play is a function of the power structure;

(f)   decisions are a function of power structure <u>and</u> power
      structure is a function of decisions.

Broadly contemplated, the economic decision-making process--and,
with the necessary adjustments, its subprocess and institutions--
involves variables which are at the same time both dependent and
independent variables. They include: individual choice, power
structure, opportunity set structure, working rules, ideology,
resource allocation, income and wealth distributions, values system, preference functions, and so on.

A.8.   The model of social decision-making articulated in terms
of power comprises one distinctive approach to one interacting
facet of a larger paradigm in which policy is related to power,
knowledge and psychology.

<u>8.a.</u>   The general interdependence relationship may be stated
as <u>follows</u>: policy is a function of power, knowledge and

psychology (in the sense that policy can be seen as dependent upon variables grouped and analyzed under these headings) and power, knowledge and psychology are a function of policy (in that the variables subsumed thereunder are themselves influenced by effective social choices.)

8.b. Although our subject here is power, it must be acknowledged that any or most decision-making phenomena can be analyzed in terms of power, knowledge or psychology and that any or most important statements made in terms of one of the three can be stated, with appropriate transformation equations or rules, in terms of either of the others.

A.9. Law (the state, government) is an instrument for the attainment of economic objectives and the economy (e.g., the market) is an object of legal control. In terms of a general interdependence relationship, economic activity and the resolution of the basic economic problems (resource allocation, income distribution, income-level determination) through the market are a partial function of the operation and policies of the legal process and the operation and policies of the legal process are a partial function of the power play (and knowledge and psychology) of economic actors. The economic (market) and legal (sub-) processes are deeply, elaborately, complexly, and subtly intertwined, with the economy a partial function of the polity and the polity a partial function of the economy. These same points can be made in terms of "public" and "private," between which there is no permanent and clear line of separation; rather, what is normally private is typically deeply grounded in state action and nominally state action is the result of actors and forces originating in the private sector and working or realized through the state. Much of this is to say that the private-sector economy and the public-sector state are institutional complexes through which individuals and subgroups, with and without official status, attempt to secure their goals. The interactions typically comprise elements of both conflict and symbiosis, with now one rising to the surface and then the other, but with both functioning to identify the structural significance of the interacting parties or institutions.

9.a.   Institutions structure power. Indeed, at any point in time they embody power and constitute the power structure. Power play or interaction among institutions is partly aimed at using institutions to change the power structure and partly to serve or secure ideal and/or material ends. With government as such an institution, and anticipating the next section, the general proposition or principle of power may be stated as:

Government is an instrument or vehicle available for the use of whomever can get into a position to control it; which has as corollaries the following:

Opportunities for gain--pecuniary profit and/or political or other advantage--accrue to those both in and out of government office who can use government successfully.

Government is an arena in which and for which various claimants or participants compete for advantage, i.e., government is an object of power play or jockeying for position.

These propositions apply, with the necessary adjustments, to all institutions whether nominally private or public. Still stated in reference to government, the critical analytical--and policy-- questions become:

Who is using government, how, and for what purposes?

What is the process through which control of government is determined over time?

Like the entire preceding analysis, these are neutral and non-pejorative propositions applicable to all governments, to all theories of the role of government, and, inter alia, to all those whose personal conceptions of the public good become or would become identified, through their control of government, with or as the social welfare function. (No small.amount of ideology and language functions to obscure the actual uses to which government is put. One of the intended consequences of the essay is to pierce the veil of the public utility institution.) Anyone's theory or conception of what government should or should not do is, in effect, his approach to the use of government. Government, subunits of government, and institutions generally are vehicles or instruments of those who determine their use and therefore are the arenas in which potential users contend for that use.

9.b. The state, therefore, may be seen as participating in several fundamental social processes. These include: (a) the resolution of conflict, the maintenance of law and order, and the protection of the existing system against consolidations of perceived antagonistic social developments; (b) the division and redivision of power in society, both within the nominally private sector and between it and the public sector, including the articulation and assignment of rights and obligations of economic significance; and (c) the provision and revision of the basic economic institutions, including the institutionalization of the economic system per se and the formation of the institutions giving substance to the system. The actually critical issues deal with on whose terms and in whose interests conflicts are resolved, law and order maintained, the system protected, the power divided and redivided, and the economic institutions provided for and revised. Government (and subunits thereof) is thus an arena for power play and an object of capture. It is an object of use by those who effectively appreciate that government has to make decisions in performing those functions and in developing those legally based economic institutions and who, accordingly, seek to have those functions performed and those institutions developed in support of their particular interests. That there is the institution and law of private property is not enough: both the institution and the law may be used to support one set of interests or another.

2.B.   Some Principles of Power

B.1.   The foregoing model has been rather baldly stated, eschewing the semantics, idealized interpretations, and other gloss with which actual institutions (especially government) are typically described by both actors and analysts. This section presents certain principles which attempt to identify fundamental elements of the economy and polity as systems of power by applying them, with the necessary adjustments, to all decision-making processes and institutions. Insofar as any of these may be considered as "laws," they are such only in the Marshallian sense, as statements of tendencies. One interesting thing about these principles is the conflict they articulate. Again, they are essentially positive descriptive propositions, lacking ideological or normative content.

Group One

1.1. Decisions are a function of the power structure (i.e., of opportunity set structure, power structure, and mutual coercion).

1.2. Power players attempt to manipulate the power structure in order to influence or control the decisions.

1.3. Power is reciprocal: the power of Alpha is checked by the power of Beta, and vice versa, when they are in the same field of power or power situation.

1.4. Institutions represent power structures and participation in decision making; institutional change means change of or defense against change of the power structure.

Group Two

2.1. Power is necessary to accomplish desired ends.

2.2. The quest for power is partially derived from the desire for particular ends.

2.3. The quest for power is partially derived from the desire for power per se (e.g., ego fulfillment or defense).

Group Three

3.1. Those with power tend to seek further power.

3.2. The fear of power leads to a desire to use power as a check on power of others. Thus actors fear power, yet use it to accomplish desired ends, including the checking of the power of others.

3.3. There are unequal perceptions of power, i.e., different persons have different (and changing) perceptions as to when "power" is involved and when not. Inadequate power perception prevents complete recognition of past and present power structures, situations, and struggles. Power used to check power is often not seen as "power," although it is sometimes understood that the power necessary to check another's power itself requires checking.

3.4. The formation of power tends to generate its own rationale for holding power, its own legitimacy, which is formulated in absolutist and exclusivist terms.

3.5. Change, particularly institutional change, tends to be evaluated primarily in terms of probable effects on power structure and/or on the use of power.

Group Four
    4.1. Coercive pressure is a function of economic and/or
political importance (tested by withholding or
threatening to withhold), capacity to organize, and
cohesiveness of organization. The capacity to organize is critical in the accumulation of power, the
formation of opportunity sets, and the exercise of
mutual coercion.

    B.2. These propositions generalize and represent a wide range
of human experience. As already indicated the phenomena which they
interpret and generalize can also be interpreted in terms of knowledge and psychology, and it is both an evidential and interpretive problem to decide which interpretation (or combination of
interpretations) is applicable to any given phenomenon. But these
propositions in terms of power not only tentatively interpret any
social phenomenon, they also point to fundamental aspects of such
phenomena insofar as power is involved. They are particularly appropriate to the public utility institution.

    3. THE PUBLIC UTILITY INSTITUTION AS A SYSTEM OF POWER

In this section, I attempt to characterize and interpret the public utility institution in terms of the foregoing approach to
power. I will do this through a sequence of what are intended to
be neutral, positive propositions. These propositions apply to
commissions and commissioners and to utilities, as well as to pol-
liticians and to consumer and other groups. Before any of these
individuals can be praised or criticized in terms of the following
propositions, an additional normative premise must be added which
is <u>not</u> intended here.

3.A. The Public Utility Institution as a Power Institution

    A.1. The public utility is a power institution in which power
is necessary and is used to influence decisions and policies, including performance in respect to income and wealth distribution;
in which effective decisions and policies as well as performance
are partially a function of the structure in which any one party's
power is constrained in one way or another by the power of other
parties; in which there is much jockeying for positions of power
and manipulation of working rules and enhanced opportunity sets
as each party-in-interest seeks to achieve its own perceived goals,
interests, and/or advantage; and which represents the uses to
which it is put by those in control.[4]
    1.a. The public utility institution [hereinafter: institu-
tion] is a subprocess of collective or public decision-making and
is characterized by choice and power. The institution structures
power and opportunity sets and is an object of power play to alter
power and opportunity sets in the interests of particular players.

1.a.i. The extant institution commits us to a particular decision-making process and pattern and logic of choice[5] dependent upon the power structure within and operative through it and the uses to which it is put.

1.a.ii. The institution is characterized by ubiquitous choice or discretion in the organization, operation and regulation of public utilities, although institutional paraphernalia and semantics obscure the choice character of the institution and its processes and results.

1.a.iii. The institution embodies a power situation and a dynamic power structure. It is at the same time both an arena in which parties contest and an object of capture and use. Its phenomena and problems are in large part those of power.

1.a.iv. Both the institution as a whole and its subunits represent concentrated economic and political power. Inevitable tension accompanies the selection and balancing of ends manifest in power play over institutional structure.

1.a.v. This institution governs the status in the larger economic decision-making process of intensively regulated privately-owned utilities [hereinafter: utilities]. By status is meant the loci and conditions of participation, encompassing the utilities' relations to other private enterprises, regulatory commissions, and courts, and most immediately to the general public in the form of material suppliers, investors, workers, and consumers.

1.a.vi. The institution governs the relative power or participation of the utility in the decision process, as well as the coordinates of its power. It also governs its exposure to the power of other economic actors, especially the relative exposure of utilities and their customers to the market (but legally based) power of the other.

A.2. Administrative or commission regulation [hereinafter: regulation] has the dual general functions of restricting opportunities considered undesirable (e.g., to charge exorbitant and discriminatory prices) and promoting opportunities considered socially desirable (e.g., fostering efficient and adequate supply of the utility's product or service). At stake is the precise meaning to be given to "socially desirable and undesirable."

A.3. Theories of rate of return ultimately involve judgment as to the opportunity set to be allowed utilities.[6] This and other general theories of regulation do not specify the particular position--in terms of power, opportunity sets, and mutual coercion-- of particular utilities, except that industries or companies so declared will receive special legal treatment. The details are worked out through the complex and continuing administration of the institution, which is to say, through the power play focusing on and through regulation as parties-in-interest jockey for power so as to enhance their respective opportunity sets.

3.B. The Institution as Total Decision-Making Process

Although it is conventional to perceive utilities and regulatory commissions as separate and distinct, albeit interacting, entities, both should be seen primarily as parts of the holistic, complex, and dynamically changing structure of power, opportunity sets, and exercise of mutual coercion that is the public utility decision process. The effective choices or policies that emerge are thus not strictly those of regulation or of utilities alone, but of the total public utility decision process, of the institution as a whole.

   B.1.   The institution includes the regulatory or administrative commissions, the utility companies, the executive branch of government, the legislature, and the courts, as well as, more narrowly, such phenomena as the chairmen of interested and powerful congressional committees, the major Washington (and state capital) law firms, the power brokers in the Office of the President (and Governor), the National Association of Regulatory Utility Commissioners (NARUC), and so on. Each of the aforementioned participants is a locus of power making choices from within its opportunity set and thereby (in part) affecting the changing aggregate structure of power and opportunity sets over time. The thrust of regulation is to impose commission participation in the management of utilities.[7] But management, in the sense of decision-making, must be ultimately perceived in terms of the total institution. Judicial review of commission action, i.e., judicial recourse or judicial activism, has long been an important element of the institution. It has articulated, defended, changed, and weakened particular rights of particular parties.[8] Commission and/or court passivism with respect to regulation does not eliminate commission (and/or court) participation in the institution but merely leads to reinforcement of decisions made elsewhere,e.g., by utilities.

   B.2.   Much effective decision-making is the result not of statutes per se but of the exercise of (i) regulator choice from within the statutory cum court framework (effective opportunity set) and (ii) regulator-regulatee interrelations and symbiosis.

   2.a.   The absence of clear and precise statutory goals reflects only in part the inability of the legislature to work out detailed policy solutions. It also signifies the effective "delegation" of discretion or power[9] to the commissions as part of the institution (and thereby the interests and pressures that work and compete through the commissions).

   2.b.   Rational decision-making would seem to require well-defined, precise, agreed-upon objectives and goals of regulation, and the absence of same in regulation has been widely lamented. But a heterogeneous institution leads to ambiguous statements of purpose and goals because of the continuing jockeying for position as parties-in-interest compete to have their particular goals become the goals of the institution and to revise the statutory goals, the intermediate ends, and the working rules in their interests. With multiple, competing goals and criteria advanced by the competing parties-in-interest, clear and consistent goals or solutions are not permanently possible,[10] as all are subject to continual revision in one corner or another of the institution.

   B.3.   Politics is a mode of governing but it is also a mode

of organizing government; likewise, regulation is the mode of
reaching goals but it is also the mode of organizing or articu-
lating goals. Regulation, like government in general, exists not
only to effectuate goals but to formulate them, and a government
or regulatory system with, or responsive to, a diffused power
structure is not likely to reach final, unambiguous goals. The institution, especially with respect to regulation, is a decision-
making process regarding its own goals.

   B.4. The open-ended complexity and power jockeying that characterize the institution reflect (i) the actuality of the dynamic
interplay within the institution seen as a decision-making process, (ii) the contingent character of the institution's power
structure, and (iii) the fact that regulation is not typically an
exogenous and unilateral exercise of unchallengeable, immovable
power, but a participatory system in which the regulated participate as legally protected parties-in-interest.[11]

3.C. Influences Upon the Regulatory System

   Any regulatory system influences and is influenced by larger
forces:[12] the market, politics, technology, and institutional adjustment.

   C.1. Commission regulation is part of a larger power structure and power situation with respect, first, to the institution
per se, and, second, to social, political, and economic power and
their interaction.[13] These larger power structures and processes
shape the organization, conduct, and consequences of regulation.
At the same time, regulation gives form to underlying conflicts
and, moreover, generates and structures pressures and interests
of its own.[14] Regulation is an object of capture and use by parties-in-interest, as a vehicle or lever for the realization of
their goals. Thus regulation is an interacting variable in a larger decision system in which other forces may work against or reinforce but will always condition the operation and substance of
regulation.

   1.a. Regulation and regulatory reform must be comprehended
within the matrix of the total institution and the total matrix
of forces that operate on and through it. Reformers often see
regulation and regulatory reform as a kind of therapy with regard
to the contradictions they perceive between private and social
interests. But the institution is only an arena in which power
players contest for position and fruits, and in which differences
in decisions and performance result from differences in powers,
structure and working rules. Both regulation and reform are parts
of a general-equilibrium system.

   1.b. How "effective" regulation has been with respect to the
ostensible objectives of regulation is a separate question. Recent research[15] suggests that the dominant power players in the
absence of regulation are dominant under regulation and that market results reflect this continued dominance, i.e., that regulation has been an alternative vehicle within the opportunity sets
of the regulated which they use to effectuate their interests.

C.2.   The concept and goal of "independent" commissions and
autonomous and objective decision-making is illusory.[16] It functions primarily as a moral restraint upon some of the rougher
edges of power play, and with uncertain results. Commission(er)s
are politically and economically significant and strategically
located; they are conduits through which pressures of mutual coercion are directed. They are both dependent and independent variables in a system of general interdependence. The jockeying for
power that marks the institution is a function of (a) the realities
of the interrelation of legal (political) and economic processes,
(b) the dynamics of institutional change, and (c) the conflicting
desiderata that (i) commission power represent a viable and "effective" force and (ii) commission power be checked by other power players both within government and in the private (but legally
protected) sector. "Independence" is illusory ultimately because
regulation is a part of a larger set of forces and power institutions. "Corruption" and "influence" have to be understood (though
not necessarily condoned) in terms of the totality of the institution and the fact that regulation both influences and is influenced by larger forces.

C.3.   Regulation is a functional equivalent to property rights
in that both are the grounds of power in structuring participation in the decision-making process.[17] Market participation by
utilities and other businesses is only within and on the basis of
the total power (including rights) structure. The historic rationale of regulation has been to "correct" the power and rights
structure, e.g., because of consumers' disadvantage, amounting to
the restriction of certain rights (of monopolization and discrimination) otherwise viable in and through private property.[18]

3.a.   A result of this is the cost-price structure, and therefore, the profit-opportunity structure delimiting the opportunity-
set structure of particular utilities (governed in part by the
theory of regulation in relation to return operative through the
institution). The institution (and especially regulation) thus
represents a particular structuring of a part of the socioeconomic
reward and incentive system. Income and wealth distribution is a
partial function of demand and supply which, in turn, is a partial
function of power in the market which, in turn, is a partial function of relative rights, including those generated by and through
regulation.

3.b.   With income and wealth distribution a partial function
of regulation, regulation itself is a function of the uses to
which regulation is put. Those who can control regulation (as with
the law of property generally) will use it to improve their own
position. Regulation is thus a system of taxation,[19] and, like
taxation, a handle which various power players can grip and use to
change income and wealth distribution in their favor.[20] Much behavior within the ambit of regulation and the institution as a
whole can be explained and predicted on the basis of intended
effects of changes in policy or organization upon income and
wealth distribution.[21] The principle of the use of government and

its corollaries applies quite specifically and forcefully to the public utility institution.

3.D.   Regulation Used by Those Who Control It

Regulation, as with government in general, is an instrument or vehicle available for the use of whoever can get into a position to control it.

D.1.   The use of the institution, including regulation, is a function of the theory given effect in its operation. If it is not one theory, it will be another. If it is not a business (management) or profit-cum-growth-oriented theory, it will be a worker, a consumer, a politician, or another, say, environmentalist-oriented theory.[22] In reality it is an amalgam of all of these; hence, the absence of clear goals; hence, too, the theory of regulation as an object of influence.

D.2.   All parties-in-interest require power in or through the institution in order to effectuate their interests and goals. They contest to acquire and exercise this power and to shape the rules governing both acquisition and exercise of power. The power structure and working rules, considered as dependent variables, effectuate the specific uses to which the institution is put, thereby functioning as independent variables with regard to performance.

2.a.   Each party-in-interest attempts to secure, maintain and strengthen its power position thereby to enhance its opportunity set vis-a-vis the others. This may be considered as the objective function which they try to maximize or as the instrumental means to further objectives such as prestige, income and wealth, and/or power as an end in itself. The history of regulation is one of parties-in-interest attempting to use regulation for their own ends. Since decisions and performance are functions of the structure of power, parties-in-interest attempt to manipulate the structure in order to effect results favorable to their own opportunity sets, and given the structure of power, the contest is over particular policies. Regulation is an arena for struggle over the distribution of government largesse in one form or another, i.e., via direct and indirect subsidies.

2.b.   All of this is rationalized in terms of power language, with the terminology used being that which will legitimize claims to power or the exercise of power[23] and which attempts to obscure the power-and-choice character of the point(s) at issue.

D.3.   The basic logic of regulation is the use of (government) power to check power--whether the latter power be that of utilities or that of firms to whom the utilities would be otherwise exposed.

D.4.   If regulation is to check power and/or the abuse of power, it remains to be decided precisely what power or what exercise of power is to be checked and by whom and for whom. Similarly, if regulation is to both restrict and promote, it remains to be decided what is to be restricted and what promoted, wherein the parties-in-interest are each to be restricted and enhanced in their opportunity sets vis-a-vis the others.

D.5. Utilities have come to dominate regulation either by
initial design, by eventual capture, or by symbiotic development.[24]
The emphasis upon restriction and promotion is primarily a function of the effective capture, and/or cooptation in one way or
another, or regulation by the ostensibly regulated, or by some of
the ostensibly regulated, i.e., the dominance by business reasoning and the interests of the regulatees.

5.a. Regulation is a system of social control, but it is also
a power system available to those in and out of government office,
to those who are able to assume and perform the functions of
social control. The uses of regulation as a system of social control must involve balancing of interests, enhancing some and inhibiting others. Regulation has become primarily an advocate for
particular regulatee interests, the interests advocated being
primarily those of some or all ostensibly regulated firms, but at
the same time it serves as a conflict-resolving social control
system.

5.a.i. The capture and/or cooptation of regulation by the
regulated is facilitated by the industry structure of much of
regulation. Highly organized industries with relatively clear
objectives have considerable advantage over the interests of consumers who possess severely limited capacity for organized action.[25]
Regulation has almost invariably become primarily an advocate of
the regulated industry.[26] It has been a vehicle for the establish-
ment and enhancement of concentrated power, an instrument for the
amassing and protection of corporate power.

5.a.ii. The business use of government regulation may be seen
as a system of corporate socialism[27] and regulation as involving
a system of taxation.[28] It is "socialism" or "welfare state" when
the largesse is for others, "promotion" when it is for business
interests.[29]

5.b. Regulation has come to perform the following regulatee-
oriented functions:

   i.   a general tendency to protect and rationalize business
        interests when those come in conflict with consumer and
        other interests;[30]
  ii.   an entrenchment function through the basic franchise or
        certification establishment of the position of the
        regulated firm(s) in the market; a tendency to lock in
        and institutionalize the company(ies), the deepest level
        of protection, antecedent to the question of market
        structure per se;
 iii.   a protection function involving the protection of market
        structure or the protection of particular industries or
        firms[31] as a system of privilege,[32] the protection of
        the extant distribution of wealth within an industry,[33]
        and the protection of economic interests from the dis-
        cipline of the market.[34] The protection function may be
        an inevitable result of the logic of regulation;[35]
  iv.   a facade function whereby the consuming public is in-
        duced to believe that government is meaningfully

restricting the power of the regulated and whereby more
stringent and consumer-oriented regulation is avoided by
intentional impotency and diversionary activity;[36]

v.   a (related) soporific function whereby public ownership
     is made out to be unnecessary, i.e., the function of
     regulation is to avoid public ownership;[37]

vi. a cartel function whereby the commission(s) polices the
     market administering the governmentally cartelized in-
     dustry to the advantage of all or the major firms in the
     industry.[38] Within the cartel and protection functions,
     there exists rivalry for shares of the cartel profits,
     often lauded as competition;[39]

vii. a scapegoat function whereby the regulatees can attempt
     to place blame for problems and failures on incompetent
     or ill-directed regulation.

5.c. The classic statement of this interpretation:

My impression would be that, looking at the matter from
a railroad point of view exclusively, [repeal of the
Interstate Commerce Act] would not be a wise thing to
undertake. . . . The attempt would not be likely to
succeed; if it did not succeed, and were made on the
ground of inefficiency and uselessness of the Commission, the result would very probably be giving it the
power it now lacks. The Commission, as its functions
have now been limited by the courts, is, or can be
made, of great use to the railroads. It satisfies the
popular clamor for a government supervision of railroads, at the same time that that supervision is almost
entirely nominal. Further, the older such a Commission
gets to be, the more inclined it will be found to take
the business and railroad view of things. It thus becomes a sort of barrier between the railroad corporations and the people and a sort of protection against
hasty and crude legislation hostile to railroad interests. . . . The part of wisdom is not to destroy
the Commission, but to utilize it.[40]

D.6. Regulation is not used solely by the regulatees; it performs functions for other parties-in-interest, especially the provision of sinecures for political parties.

D.7. Regulation is primarily responsive to those interests
with whom it has developed symbiotic relations (so that the idea
of capture may be less descriptive than cooptation which may be
mutual).[41] Regulatees come to prefer the relative certainty of
regulation to the vicissitudes of competition, and regulators come
to define their own identity in terms of the industry regulated
(and, of course, this identification may be a foregone conclusion
if the regulator is associated with the regulated industry prior
to or after commission service). The regulators therefore see
their role as important only or primarily vis-a-vis an antagonist

whom they typically prefer not to antagonize; each, that is to say,
gains from the deference cum support provided by the other. "A
licensing agency inevitably comes to identify the public interest
with its own authority and its own authority with the regulated
industry."[42] (There are, of course, many regulators who escape
such symbiosis and capture; but they are not typical, and if they
were typical the system would work rather differently.) In this
psychic reciprocity, regulation is by far the weaker (and the less
well rewarded) partner, notwithstanding the ostensible state
authority which it carries--given the pressures of power, career,
prestige, and money operating on the regulators (which may seem
paradoxical, since in replacing whatever diffusion of power was
possible without regulation, regulation may cement consumer disadvantage).[43] Among other things, the regulators cater to the
fears of the regulatees, and the regulatees cater to the desire
for deference of the regulators. At the same time that extant
regulation is lauded it is criticized as sometimes nonunderstand-
ing.[44] A similar routine is followed in support of state regulation when federal regulation is deemed hostile, wrong, or beyond
capture or cooptation; but federal regulation is supported when
state regulation is inefficient or unresponsive. Typically, a
symbiotic relation exists between state regulation and industry
versus federal regulation.

D.8.   The chief behavioral principle followed by all parties-
in-interest, including commission regulators, is the pursuit of
that which will maintain and strengthen their interest as they
see it, with their interest generally reduceable to pecuniary and/
or political advantage and/or psychic security. Thus a maximizing
postulate is generally appropriate, with the qualifications (a)
that different parties-in-interest tend to have significantly
different substantive situations and goals; (b) that goals, preferences, or objective functions are complex and changing, especially in important details; (c) that different particular parties
may have different chains of normative reasoning or differently
specified general goals; and (d) that different modes of rationality may be followed.[45]

8.a.   Regulators attempt to maximize, in addition to their
income, their status and power, perhaps in short, their career
gradient and level, typically by increasing the degree and scope
of their authority. This is a constrained maximization situation,
since there are costs involved in extending their power, e.g.,
hostility among the regulated firms.

8.a.i.   Regulatory power tends to (seek its own) increase as
the extant limits thereto are perceived as barriers to the effectuation of whatever (and whosever) goals are adopted by the commission.[46] A tension exists between the tendency for regulators to
seek an increase in their power and the symbiotic balance--which
is in no small part a balance between their demands and those of
the regulated.

8.a.ii.   Commissions tend to seek security, to minimize oppo-
sition or criticism, to avoid major conflicts, to pursue safe
objectives and to be preoccupied with details of regulation and

minutiae of cases.[47] They manifest the psychology of bureaucracy: fear, defensiveness, evasiveness, secrecy, etc. The personal variable is always important and sometimes crucial.[48]

8.a.iii. Regulation is a haven for regulators. It represents an important phase of their career pattern, their identity, their income and prestige source. Regulators are regulation-minded since regulation is their speciality--and industry-mindedness is as much an effect of this as a cause.[49] Regulators want to protect the system of regulation, to protect the image of regulation, and to condition the public to accept the work of the extant system of regulation.[50] Often with a clear identification with the regulated industries,[51] the regulatory commissions develop their own interests, which are pursued in the name of the public interest.

8.b. Judicialization is a function of (a) the passive role of commissions; (b) the attempt to gain prestige and status by emulating the courts; (c) the capture of regulation by the bar, seeking to abort any challenge to the common law mode of governmental decision-making, as well as projecting their own mode of rationality--and, of course, the predominance of lawyers; and (d) concern with (and impact of) procedural and constitutional requirements.[52]

8.c. Utilities, commission(er)s and the bar are not the only beneficiaries of regulation. The executive and the legislative branches (on the federal level, the president and the committee chairmen in Congress especially) also treat regulation as an object of capture and/or use, as a partner in symbiosis, for a variety of economic and political purposes, e.g., political power brokering, favoritism (part of the political incentive and reward system to which many commission appointees are indebted), effectuation of particular goals or policies in favor of consumers, reformers, environmentalists, utilities, financial interests, etc. Consumer and other groups would use regulation to effect a minimization approach to rate of return and to utility status generally,[53] in part to limit the costs to themselves of utility services and to enhance their opportunity sets.

8.d. With regulation fundamentally involved in the formulation of power and opportunity-set structures and the distribution of income and wealth, as both a dependent and independent variable, much regulatory behavior is subject to analysis "on the basis of the effects of changes in policy upon the distribution of income and wealth."[54] The research problem is to penetrate the institution's decision process and get behind the language and rationales of official decision statements, for the stipulated or ostensible purposes typically ignore, and sometimes mask, the real purposes which must be traced back to power play and intended income-and-wealth effects.[55]

D.9. The institution, and the behavioral principle applicable to all activity with respect to it, have analogs in all systems of economics and politics, e.g., command economies. The particular form taken in the U.S. is a function of the dominant and ubiquitous business system. It is (a) a direct, albeit sometimes subtle, restraint on the institution and on regulation per se, (b) the

origin of symbiotic relations, (c) the origin of the dilemma of
promotion versus restriction, and (d) asymmetrical in its pattern
of pressure upon commissions. In a business society, the dominant
influence on regulation is the power structure and mentality of
business and property.[56] Consumers and consumer groups also behave
as maximizers, or economic men: like unions and companies, consumers want to enhance their opportunity sets in ways and/or for
purposes conditioned by the business system.

D.10. The uses to which regulation has been put, and the
jockeying for position, have been many and varied. The demand for
particular rights, for a particular theory of regulation (e.g.,
utility- or consumer-oriented), for particular objectives, is a
demand for regulation and for a particular use to which the institution (regulation) is to be put. To want "better" regulation is
to want regulatory attention to one's values and priorities, to
want a restructuring of regulatory priorities and of the power
structure of regulation as a means thereto.

10.a. The uses have varied over time and between both regulatory areas (commissions and/or industries) and beneficiaries,
but have included: the use of the courts and the property mentality to protect what have become identified as established
rights; the manipulation of legal standing to increase or restrict
opportunity sets through access or denial of access to the courts;[57]
allowing capitalization of monopoly income generated by legal
licensing through sale of franchises; the use of eminent domain
principles (the fair return on fair value formula) as a check on
regulation and a defense of status quo and monopoly rights (including the potential if not actuality of protecting monopoly
returns if carried to logical conclusion) and as defense against
the use of competition as regulatory policy; budgetary limits upon
commissions used as a lever to reduce their effective power and
opportunity sets and thereby to "discourage vigorous and adven-
turesome administration";[58] reliance upon a wholly-owned manufacturing subsidiary and its prices although exempt from regulation;
consumer representation on utility boards as a substitute for
(effective) regulation; deliberate and explicit protection of the
market and income position of one firm or set of firms as opposed
to others; prevention against exorbitant and discriminatory rates,
or of one set of differential rates as opposed to another; primary reliance upon businessmen and business consultants in regulatory hearings in formulating regulatory policy; the role of
personal economic, political and/or career advantage of particular
individuals, such as commissioners, members of the legislature,
power brokers in the executive branch and the business and other
beneficiaries of such brokering; decisions not to prosecute or to
enter into consent decrees (as opposed to either an impartial or
vigorous enforcement of law);[59] approval of pricing to subsidize
high-cost firms; buying or otherwise capturing political machinery
to influence granting of franchises, desirable terms of regulation,
prices, rate of return, etc.; the use of "grandfather" clauses
coupled with the nonissuance of new licenses; hidden subsidies;
retardation of technological innovation; the role of major law

firms in writing statutes at the behest of clients for congressional submission;[60] and so on.

10.b. The power play has also been varied and has included:
the use of the courts as a weapon through the creation of delay
(by companies, by environmentalist groups, etc.);[61] jockeying for
inclusion in (and exclusion from) regulation; power play over
commission-staff relations;[62] interaction between members of Congress and the regulatory agencies, with the former representing
in one way or another the interests of utility companies, consumer
groups, environmentalist groups, or others; power play over the
relative roles of state versus federal agencies, and of commissions versus courts; the formation and use of NARUC to promote
state regulatory interests as opposed to federal; the use of "crisis!" cries to turn regulation to advantage by swamping other con-
siderations; bringing cases to test how far the law (the courts)
will go, affirmatively or negatively; and so on. Much nonutility-
regulation activity of government has been used to achieve the
same functional results of regulation for the advantage of particular interest groups.[63]

10.c. The specific uses to which regulation is put is a function of the asymmetrical access to or pressure upon the commission,
and the enormous opportunity and incentive to wheel and deal,
i.e., to manipulate the political and economic environment, enjoyed
by the strategically located concentrated economic power of utilities. All of this is facilitied by the use of economic and other
constituents for political advantage and the use of politicians by
economic and other interests.

D.11. Most phenomena and problems of regulation (and the institution as a whole) are a consequence of the fact that the logic
of the institution, in addition to the very important factor of
organizing activity, is very much a matter of the use of power as
a check on power. The use of power through government typically
has two facets; first, the control or restriction of certain loci
of power, and second, the protection or enhancement of other loci
of power. The desire that power be checked by having power widely
diffused (or, say, by institutional contervailance) does not
always mean the destriction of power--but rather its taming.
Both the benefits of the use of power and the restraint of power
are desired;[64] and both desiderata often conflict. Although performance of governmental institutions is typically evaluated in
terms of efficiency and substantive goal realization rather than
power diffusion, the organization of government often aims at the
division of power to prevent abuse of power (always a subjective
matter), and not to produce efficiency.

11.a. Unchecked power (say, utilities without regulation or
"independent" commissions) necessary to achieve certain purposes
must be juxtaposed to checked power (say, regulated utilities, or
"nonindependent" commissions) necessary to achieve certain other
purposes. Concentrated power is necessary to get action, yet
narrow concentration of power is feared. Diffusion of power may
mean either no check on power or an inability to get things done.[65]
Criticism of the power of utilities is often coupled with criticism

that utilities are not more socially responsible or doing more
for society, i.e., assuming more power. Both centralization and
decentralization may produce tyranny;[66] and economic giants may
visit damage both by intentionally or unintentionally smothering
lesser powers.

11.b. Notwithstanding the tendency for regulation to expand,
the problems with which regulation has to deal may involve greater social space and authority requirements than are enjoyed by
regulatory commissions. A criterion of power management is to
have authority and/or jurisdiction coextensive with the scope of
the problem; but perhaps all problems can be infinitely expanded,
and the principle of the necessity of power to accomplish goals
conflicts with (a) the desire to have power check power and (b)
diseconomies of scale of decision-making.

11.c. The diffusion of power may mask the concentration of
power (e.g., diffusion of power in one respect or area representing absence of effective check to concentrated power in another
respect or area). There is conflict between strategies of (a)
further concentration of power and (b) further deconcentration
of power, in order to produce "meaningful" checks on power—which
are a function of perception of power, empirical ends-means relationships, and subjective evaluation of power holders. Policies
involving the increased effectiveness of regulation through concentration of power may conflict with the desideratum of having regulation responsive to consumers—and be more amenable to capture
or cooptation by those who can influence the officials representing the new concentration of power.

11.d. A major problem is that of how regulation can be "improved" if regulation is controlled by the regulated. This is related to the problem of whether huge, politically influential
business empires can be effectively controlled, which is the problem of extending government control when government is already
primarily subservient to the intended regulatees; which is part
of the larger problem of whether an institution can be at the
same time "the advocate of a partial interest and the community's
agent for reconciling that partial interest with the larger interest."[67] Regulation both generates and accelerates conflict,
and focuses and channels conflict. Power checked by power means a
dynamic interacting juxtaposition of opportunity sets, with no
necessary antecedent capacity to predict consequences of such interaction.

D.12. With the institution's effective policies being a function of power, knowledge and psychology, there are other psychological facets as well as knowledge factors which go beyond the
foregoing.

12.a. With respect to psychology, the foregoing attention
to a complex maximizing behavioral principle, the processes of
regulator identification with the interests of the regulatees, the
importance of bureaucratic mentality, and the relevance of different modes of rationality do not exhaust the psychology of regulation. Both objective and subjective factors operate in the market
and in regulation: for example, the public's view of utilities as

a relatively safe (or unsafe) investment will affect the cost of capital. What people expect from regulation, and from utilities, is important with respect to the demand for and practice of regulation, and such expectations are the object of symbol manipulation by utilities,[68] among others. The problem is not evil businessmen but the "excesses" (a subjective matter, like "abuse" of power) of the more-or-less normal drive to get ahead. The commission(er)s' own view of their role is important: many more readily identify with the role of steering stable growth of the regulated industry than with the imposition of negative restrictions. Problems of image and protocol are very serious in the interaction between various parties-in-interest.[69] Identification with the regulatees is facilitated by (a) the established position of the regulated firms; (b) the tendency to share the concerns of groups with whose problems they become familiar;[70] and (c) the proximity of personable company advocates, which has an insidious effect, particularly when those advocates are diligently attentive to the "commissioners' preferences, concerns, weaknesses, and alliances."[71]

12.b. With respect to knowledge, since policy is a partial function of people's definition of reality and of values, power players attempt to influence such knowledge in order to influence policy. To influence policy, and to influence relative power positions, they attempt to manipulate information flow, to influence what people see as abuse, what they expect from government and from utilities, and what they instinctively perceive as, e.g., the "power company,"[72] as well as the information relevant to the making of knowledgeable decisions about rates. Companies complain of "uninformed" regulation, but not only does this mean primarily regulation not to their liking (and functions to discredit and disengage possible activist consumer-oriented regulation) but also their trying to keep the necessary data concerning company operations from the commissions. Utilities manipulate information flow and selectively release and channel information to suit their purposes, especially on the state level,[73] taking advantage of the fact that "the companies remain the repositories of the financial information and of the technical knowledge required for any effective control or regulation of their operations."[74]

12.c. Many parties-in-interest maintain a conventional pretense of finality and inevitability of regulatory decision, obscuring the policy, choice, or discretion character of decision.[75] This absolutist position is part of the legitimation and sanctioning process.[76] There is a fundamental semantics of policy, perhaps typified by the term "public interest," which "as used by regulatory agencies . . . has become bureaucratic cant . . . invoked as a justification for whatever action is felt desirable or expedient at the moment without much more meaning than social banalities such as 'pleased to meet you' or 'very truly yours,'"[77]

12.d. Since policy as a function of knowledge is dependent upon, inter alia, information flow, the problem arises of from whose point of view is information to be developed and publicized, which is to say, whose values are to govern the design of

information systems and the management of information flow.[78] The
forces operating, the opportunities available, and the degree of
sophistication of practice in this connection are highly asymmetrical as between the parties-in-interest. Although consumer sov-
ereignty would seem to sanction and indeed mandate education of
the consumer to enable the best informed and best judging consumer
(the realization of the knowledge assumption of economic theory
and ideology), many industry forces operate to keep the consumer
uninformed and sometimes misinformed.

3.E.   Problem of Structure-Results

E.1.   The quest for power may be an end in itself but for most
people it is instrumental to the realization of particular (even
general) ends; and power institutions, such as the public utility
institution, may be designed and evaluated in terms either of the
structure of power per se and/or the performance results of the
institution(as ambiguous and difficult of assignment as they are).
In the design and evaluation of regulatory systems, accordingly,
there is a dilemma of structure versus results: designers and
evaluators may be more interested in the structure of regulation,
in the structure of power, or in the specific operating results
or impact upon the utility(ies). Regulation may be designed to
produce particular results, and if so then the problem of what or
whose results must be confronted; or regulation may be designed
in terms of principles of organizational design independent of
specific results with the understanding that whatever results are
produced by the designed structure are held to be presumptively
desirable or optimal, and, if so, then the problem of which or
whose principles of design must be confronted. Decisions may be
evaluated in terms of criteria of results independent of power
structure or they may be evaluated in terms of criteria of power
structure independent of operating results or impact. Structure
may be used to justify results and/or results may be used to justify structure. Most discussions jump from consideration of structure to results and back again, as power players follow strategies
of pursuing what they consider to be their short- and long- term
advantages.
     E.2.   The problem of regulation versus deregulation involves
the dilemma of structure versus results. The results of an unregulated market may be presumed optimal or the results of regulation may be presumed optimal, in each case a priori; or each
alternative may be evaluated in terms of specific desired operating results or utility performance. In all discussions of regulation, deregulation, consumer participation in regulatory proceedings particular structural and/or procedural arrangements, etc.,
some assumption as to the resolution of the dilemma of structure
versus results must be made.
     E.3.   Conclusions as to optimality necessarily presume, and
are specific to, some antecedent articulation and assignment of
rights or power, i.e., some assumption as to whose interests shall
be counted in the attainment of optimality of how much they shall

count. Although the models of economic analysis presume some structure of rights, and conclusions of economic optimality must be
given in terms of antecedently specific rights or power positions,
in the real world of regulation, much power play is over the
rights or power structure, i.e., over whose interests shall count.
The relative recommendatory force of the results of competition
(unregulated market) vis-a-vis regulation depends upon some assumption as to the propriety of the power and rights structures in
each case—with regulation serving as a functional equivalent to
property rights in structuring power.

E.4.   The problem of the design and reform of regulatory systems and institutions generally is how to structure power so that
those in authority will attempt to realize the values of the
parties involved, when very identification and weighting of the
values will depend upon the structure of power. Power structure
and rights are a function of values <u>and</u> values are a function of
power structure and rights.

4.   CONCLUSIONS

The purpose of this essay has been to present a model or paradigm
of power and to interpret the public utility institution, and
especially regulation, in its terms. The essay is intended to be
descriptive, not evaluative. The aim here has been to develop a
new interpretive paradigm or approach, to interpret old phenomena
in new terms, to take a neutral, positive approach to the institution, and to stress the implications of a particular theory of
power and its principles.

The public utility institution is a power institution; its
operation and performance should be understood as a function of
power (as well as knowledge and psychology).

The public utility institution is a particular organization of
economic cum political power and illustrates both the insepara-
bility of economic and political power, and the fundamental interrelations between legal (political) and economic processes.

The public utility institution serves most distinctively those
in control of it, those in a position to use it, those inside who
can and do use it, and those outside who try and can use it as a
lever. Like any power institution, it is a vehicle for those who
can control it. The historic or conventional use of the institution is taken for granted in most discussions; though the institution does not enable or provide equal opportunity to those with
different uses in mind and is not neutral with regard to either
the status quo, the parties-in-interest, or the alternative uses
to which it is or can be put.

The attempts by all parties, including the regulatees, to use
regulation is placed in perspective (a) as part of the total decision process encompassed by the institution and (b) as a manifes-
tation of the principle of the use of government, its corollaries

and the other principles of power, applied to public utility
regulation.

The interesting research problem is not how well regulation
performs the functions which rationalize its existence but what
forces govern what uses are in fact made of regulation.

The public utility institution is a conflict-resolution and
activity-organizing process and not a solution in and of itself.
The public utility institution structures power and is itself an
object of power play.

The public utility institution is different from more-or-less
ordinary business, yet they have much in common: both are institutional arrangements within which and over which the same principles of power work out. The "problems" of public utility regulation are manifestations of expected results of power situations
and the interrelation of legal and economic processes, as well as
the complexities (typically of a general equilibrium character)
of collective decision-making.

In one respect the problem of design is that of harnessing
self-interest, reinforcing social and inhibiting antisocial pro-
pensities and behavior. But the critical problem is the identification of what is social and what is antisocial. The public utility
institution is a process not only of harnessing but of identifying
what is social and antisocial, and the institution itself is part
of the system, such that it too may have or be used to produce
both social and antisocial results, in each case depending on an
uncertain mix of objective and subjective interpretive and evaluative factors but always in an open-ended general interdependence
system.

EPILOGUE

Because of its somewhat novel approach and perspective, several
aspects of this essay can be expected to generate concern. I would
like, in the interest of efficiency in discourse, to deal with my
responses to these anticipated concerns here.

1. I would have preferred that the argument be expressed in
operational terms with hypotheses subject to testing and refuta-
tion. However, some subjects are not now and may never be readily
amenable to operationalism; their importance is such that we ought
not to let our methodology dictate an exclusion of such subjects
from attention.

The power paradigm presented here does not pretend to provide
a substitute for other paradigms but rather a supplementary fundamental perspective. It stresses the necessity to comprehend the
power relations and power play found in the genesis, development,
operation, and regulation of the public utility institution. It
stresses the necessity of analyzing the forces and factors which
make the institution what it does in fact become, whereas the conventional thrusts of the legal and economic paradigms are often

used to embody (or obscure) particular theories as to what the
institution should be.

One of the uses to which a power paradigm should be put is the
construction of hypotheses which will provide, upon verification,
more solid knowledge of the public utility institution. I acknowledge and stress the difficulties involved in generating an operational definition of power. Further, most if not all of the existing operational definitions of power are limited and incomplete,
each ignoring or abstracting from other important dimensions or
facets of power. The essay thus generally stresses the importance
of a direct confrontation with <u>power</u> in understanding public
utilities and regulation and in predicting relevant behavior.

2. The paper's positive, neutral description of the institution in terms of power cannot lead to specific policy conclusions
and recommendations. To answer such questions as how much power
is too much, or whether some institutional arrangements are better
than others would require an additional normative premise. No such
normative premise(s) are included (at least intentionally) in the
paper.

Any particular normative view as to what the institution
should be is but one of several theories competing to govern the
actual control of the institution. Institutional analysts must
investigate these competing theories as so many inputs into the
process of institutional evolution. Normative analysis can presume the propriety of some theory of the institution; positive
analysis must treat all such theories as so many different approaches competing for influence or control.

Further research needs to be undertaken as to the differences
between power in different systems, though I would suggest that
the general model and principles of power developed in this essay
should apply across systems. One problem is that different persons
have different identifications as to what is a matter of power:
used pejoratively, power is what we do not like, and what we do
like is simply virtue.

Some might see a Machiavellian twist to all this. However, the
usual anti-Machiavellian proposition, namely, that ends should not
justify means, is literally not correct. Valuation by ends is the
only way by which means may be justified. What the anti-Machiavellian injunction really signifies is that we should not justify a
means by one end alone, that we should evaluate it in the light of
other, competing ends as well. In any event, from the policy analyst's neutral perspective, power must be analyzed as such, with
a minimum of wishful thinking and without identifying the institution in question with one of several possible theories of the
institution when the objective of the analysis is to understand
how the institution evolves and operates.

3. When I emphasize the utilities' domination of the institution, it is with the understanding that power is decision-making
participation; it is neither total nor absolute but relative or
reciprocal. Moreover, power is a neutral term, however hard it is
to measure. Some institutions are seen as depriving people of

power and others are seen as establishing power, but all institutions do both. Most phenomena in the world of social policy,
including the world of utilities, are not the direct result of the
power play and strategies of any one player but of the interaction
of many players, with many unanticipated and unplanned consequences
or results. To say that utilities dominate the institution does
not mean that the bond or stock market cannot treat their securities less favorably than utility executives would prefer, nor
does it mean that commissions will grant the exact amount of rate
increase for which the companies petition. It does mean that the
institution operates very differently than it would if regulation
were dominated by consumer types like Nicholas Johnson or Ralph
Nader.

4.   The emphasis in this essay is on power, with some attention to knowledge and psychology and their interaction. I certainly
acknowledge such things as (a) the role of psychological change,
for example, through changing personnel in an office or position;
and (b) the heterogeneity of commissioners with respect to their
propensity for symbiotic participation or entrapment--although all
are constrained by and must come to terms with the "system." Furthermore, my analysis includes such things as (a) the learning of
preferences and perceptions, and (b) the noble and ignoble uses
of power. But, although both "interests" and power usage are influenced by such qualities as love, honor, national character, and
altruism, there are at least the following points to be made.
First, there are conflicting definitions and substances of policies ensconced under the rubric of "love." Second, scarcity implies the necessity of choice even in a discourse on "love," ergo
the necessity of decision-making and power as contemplated herein.
Thus the use of "love" in seeming juxtaposition to "power" only
provides a more palatable terminology: "love" becomes only another
framework within which issues are articulated and fought out, and
neither a definitive and conclusive substance immediately and un-
equivocally applicable to policy nor a calculus yielding unequi-
vocal policy conclusions.

5.   I realize that the problem posed by the manageability of a
general interdependence theory of power is large and frustrating,
and I understand the attractiveness of the partial equilibrium
type of alternative. However, I am not convinced that partial
equilibrium models are the answer or the exclusive solution. The
role of the general interdependence model, as I see it, is intended to reinforce the importance of the fact of the open-ended
dynamics of the institution under study. One may desire parameters
and specifically defined partial equilibrium functions so as to
avoid the frustration of infinite regress, but the use of partial
equilibrium models is highly deceptive: they presume certain
givens which govern or influence the results of the model when in
the real world they are themselves both independent and dependent
variables, i.e., objects of capture and manipulation. Most partial
equilibrium models in economics are less efficient and manageable
and more presumptive--and presumptive on matters and/or in ways
that make the analysis no longer positive but normative (though)

not always conspicuously so).

6. I am receptive to investigating the interstices and connections between the legal and power paradigms and between the
economic and power paradigms. I think that the interrelations between legal and economic processes are far more important and complex than ideology and received models have permitted us to see
and I welcome their investigation in a positive way. The essay
suggests that the interstice between the legal and economic paradigms can and should be explored in terms of power.

7. I readily acknowledge the tautological character of the
power paradigm. Tautology is a characteristic of all paradigms
and pervades our thought. The economic paradigm is thus similarly
tautological. What distinguishes the economic from the power paradigm is not tautology but the former's presumptive, partial-equi-
librium approach. Thus the proposition that the market channels
power in efficient ways, which so readily emanates from welfare
economics, is tautological by virtue of having "efficient" depend
upon the structure of power and is presumptive in ignoring the
forces and factors that govern whose power will be given effect
through the market--functioning in effect to sanction the status
quo power structure. It is precisely this question which the power
paradigm explores--and does so without presuming, implicitly or
explicitly, the propriety of any structure of power or uses.

8. Although the Pareto-optimality analysis can be used to
analyze outcomes, seeking out opportunities for mutual benefit
which are not presently realized, such Pareto-optimal solutions
or adjustments must be recognized as being specific to a particular power structure, with their recommendatory force contingent
upon the propriety of that power structure.

COMMENTS by Mark V. Pauly

Professor Samuels's essay is a piece of ammunition in the growing
arsenal of what one might call the "counterrevolutionary" school
of public utility regulation. This view is an explicit reaction
to what Demsetz in "Information and Efficiency: Another Viewpoint"
(Journal of Law and Economics [April 1969], pp. 1-22) has called
the "grass is always greener" fallacy. That fallacy arises when
people conclude from the observation that in a particular case actual market performance for some reason falls short of theoretical
Pareto optimality, that government ought to intervene to improve
things. The non sequitur in this argument really has two aspects:
first, the implicit assumption that theoretical Pareto optimality
ought to be achieved and second, the assumption that if given the
power actual governmental institutions will obtain improvements,

will do the "right" things.

What little theory and evidence we do have about how governmental agencies or commissions operate with respect to public utility regulation serves to reinforce our suspicion that governments will not necessarily, or even usually, do the right thing. What Professor Samuels and others, mainly at the University of Chicago, are telling us is that, when normative content is added, not only will government agencies not do what economists think is right, they will do even worse than muddle through in a kind of confused but benign way. They may well actually conspire (explicitly or implicitly) with the regulated industry to do the "wrong" things, things so wrong that society would be better off with no regulation and a little market failure than with the kind of regulation we get. And the failure of regulation, they tell us, is due not to evil men but to institutional arrangements themselves.

Samuels's analysis builds on this foundation in two ways. First, it attempts to provide a theory, based on a notion of power, of why governments, agencies, and regulated firms behave the way they do. Second, it closes the circle by telling us that not only do institutions behave the way they do because of the distribution of political power, but also that the actual form of those institutions is itself an outcome of the prior distribution of power. In my remarks I shall refer to each of these points. I shall comment upon the theory of political behavior implicit in Samuels's analysis. And I shall discuss the implications for economics and economists of a theory of institution-formation of the sort he suggests.

Let me say at the beginning that I find myself in a somewhat uncomfortable position. At base, I agree with the thrust of the arguments of the Samuels-Chicago type. Economists have been bemused for too long by the romantic view of regulation as an actual attempt to set prices equal to marginal cost, when as recent studies of the history of the formation of the ICC have shown, these "efficiency" justifications apparently had little or nothing to do with the real purpose of the introduction of regulation. They were only after-the-fact rationalizations; the real purpose, stated baldly, was a redistribution of income or spoils from the general public to existing "regulated" firms, which could only be achieved if the coercive power of government could be harnessed to maintain cartel stability and to prevent competitive interlopers from entering. The normative theory of regulation is worthless as description. Yet there are, I think, some important deficiencies in the alternative theories which have been proposed. My discussion of these deficiencies should not, however, be interpreted as a basic disagreement with the essential ideas of the counterrevolution.

A THEORY OF POWER

The basic message behind Samuels's theory of power, as applied to public utility regulation, is (I take it) that the outcomes of that regulation are the consequences of the distribution of power among the agents. Since power is defined as the capacity to affect decisions, so far we only have a tautology--that things happen in a particular way because the distribution of power is such that they must happen that way. But not all tautologies are useless, and this one has a very salutary use in reminding us that the outcomes of regulatory decisions are not necessarily those produced by an economist-king armed with good intentions, a knowledge of cost and demand functions, and "P = MC" emblazoned on his escutcheon. Instead, the decisions are made by men maximizing somthing which is not necessarily (even) a welfare-weighted sum of individual utilities; rather, they maximize their own private goals.

But to add positive content to the theory, one needs to know at least two things: (a) how power is distributed, and (b) how it is exercised within a particular institutional context. In his outline at least Samuels is very vague. There are some hints from time to time about the meat that might be packed on the bones, but it takes a good deal of search to find these morsels. We are told that coercive pressure depends on the capacity to organize, and, further, that highly organized industries have an advantage over disorganized consumers. Obviously true, but where is the answer to the questions of why firms are organized and consumers disorganized, or of whether firms are always better organized than consumers (e.g., the Army vs. the uniform manufacturers)? I think the answer to these questions (and it is one of the few rudiments of an economic theory of political action) can be found in the work of Downs, Olson, and others. They note that the benefits per member of an organization are likely to be smaller the more potential benefitters there are, while the cost per member of organization is likely to increase as size increases. Thus airlines organize while travelers do not because each airline hopes to get a relatively large share of the benefit from industry action, while each traveler gets a miniscule share of the loss of benefit from that action. Even though summed damages to all consumers may exceed benefits to firms, organization of consumers may not occur.

We are also told that the vagueness economists find so exasperating in the "principles" used by regulators and courts to judge or justify actions is not just a function of the complexity of the task; vagueness is essential to permitting the exercise of power. Here again one searches for more. Are there differences in vagueness across regulated industries that might reflect differences in the distribution of power? Can't language and principles be "too vague," too arbitrary? But how much is too much? And wouldn't an industry with enough power prefer a system of actual rules (whether explicit or not) as opposed to one of ad hoc decisions?

Finally, and perhaps most importantly, we get only hints, not really an answer, to the question posed earlier in the essay: why do regulators behave the way they do? They do so because the regulatees have power, which can produce a bedfellow relationship. But does it sometimes do so, but not always, and not to the same

extent? Samuels notes that "there are, of course, many regulators
who escape such symbiosis and capture but they are not typical."
But why do such men exist? Is their existence a consequence of the
institutional arrangements in their industries, of the process by
which they were selected, or what? If these questions could be
answered, then one would <u>really</u> have a theory of power, in the
sense of a theory which yields predictions that could be refuted
by evidence. As Samuels's theory stands in the essay, it does not
meet this test, for he could claim that any outcome is a result of
some distribution of power. He could claim this because he has not
added the critical theoretical links between power and outcomes,
which specify which outcomes are predicted in which circumstances
from which distributions of power.

There seem also to be some hints that what Samuels has in mind
is not a theory of equilibrium in the distribution of political
power, but, rather, a theory to describe the dynamics or the process of acquisition of power once some initial distribution is
given, without any explanation of why the initial distribution is
what it is. But even here we still need some parameters; it cannot
be true, if one is to have a theory that explains anything, that
everything depends on everything else. There must be some fundamental structure which governs the transfer of power over time
from or to a particular group. A description of what these parameters might be, let alone a rigorous analysis of them, is wholly
absent from the essay in its present form.

There are two other comments I would like to make on Samuels's
theory of the political process. The first relates to the question
of when regulation in the interests of a particular industry is
likely to occur. In almost all industries there is some degree of
competition, more than one firm, or potential competition, or
competition from firms producing similar products in other industries. That means that there will always be a conflict, in the
sense that "industry benefit" and "firm benefit" will not necessarily be identical. It is possible, I think, that competition
here could operate as it does in a pure market to modify some of
the deleterious effects of conspiracy of power. The interesting
question is whether and when this kind of competition will work to
destroy cartel behavior, or, on the other hand, when regulation
can be used to maintain existing cartels. While it is probably
true that government intervention is necessary to make cartels
stable, it certainly is not true that government intervention is
sufficient for cartel stability, and one would like to know what
the set of sufficient conditions is.

Samuels specifically eschews normative economics. But I believe
as apparently he does not, that normative economics can be useful
in providing some hints as to where a positive theory should lead.
There are a number of comments in his essay, and other similar
ones, that regulation based on power involves economic inefficiency. The existence of economic inefficiency, by definition, means
that there is some course of action which can lead to mutual benefit which is not being followed. The positive questions then are
what are the mutual benefits and why are they not being obtained?

For example, where government regulation is used to stabilize a
monopoly, it would certainly be possible and worthwhile for the
general public to "buy off the monopolist," paying the present
value of his profit stream, in return for his agreement to operate in a competitive manner. That this does not usually happen may
be due to several causes: it may be too costly for consumers to
get together, it may be impossible to police agreements not to
behave monopolistically, or it may not be feasible to prevent
monopolists from reabsorbing "power."

A THEORY OF INSTITUTIONS

Samuels also intends to provide us with the rudiments of a theory
of institutions. If power, whatever that term may mean, explains
everything, then we really have no need of a theory of institutions, since institutions--whether or not regulation is performed
by an appointed commission, or an elected body, etc.--do not have
any effect on final outcome. But it may well be that institutions
do matter, and if they do, there is some usefulness in both the
positive theory, designed to explain the effects of different institutions on outcomes and what might be called a quasi-positive
theory, whose purpose is to explain the existence of institutional
forms as a response of mutual striving for mutual benefit. Finally,
there is the pure normative question of which sets of institutions,
given some initial distribution of power and individual preferences, are more likely to lead to outcomes which are efficient in
the economic sense.

     To the first question, Samuels gives only the answer that the
emergence of institutions depends upon the prior distribution of
power, and its exercise. I suppose this answer would imply that
there is no reason to suspect that institutions which provide
mutual benefit will emerge; it all depends on power. Here again,
we have an explanation which is really no explanation, only a
label for our ignorance.

     On the last question, Samuels specifically avoids any answer.
That is unfortunate, in my view, for I suspect that a "positive
Pareto Optimal" theory of the formation of institutions in the
public utility area might provide some useful insights, just as it
has provided some useful insights in public finance. For example,
Buchanan has shown that the progressive income tax can be justified on the basis of self-interest, without recourse to redistri-
butional explanations, if individuals are risk givers and uncertain
about their future incomes. Some similar sort of theory might be
possible to explain why commissions follow quasi-legal procedure,
why book value is used as the basis for determining rate of return,
why laws and procedures of commissions are often ad hoc, or why
service aspects of outputs of regulated industries are ignored by
commissions.

     I have the same sort of difficulty with Samuels's theory of
institutions as I had with his theory of political behavior. I am

unable to determine exactly what is exogenous in Samuels's theory.
There must be something exogenous, for if A is a function of B and
B a function of A <u>at least</u> the functional relationship must be
defined for the system to have a unique and stable solution; that
is, for the theory to explain anything. But we are never told what
these functional relationships are. Instead we get such statements
as "the power structure and working rules, considered as dependent
variables, effectuate the specific uses to which the institution
is put, thereby functioning as independent variables with regard
to performance." This sort of theory does not seem to be all that
one might hope for. Samuels's argument seems to assert that in-
stitutions in period $\underline{t}$ determine the distribution of power in $\underline{t}$ +
$\underline{1}$ which in turn determines the institutional arrangement $\underline{t}$ + $\underline{2}$,
and so forth. If we then ask why the distribution of power is what
it is at the present time, we are involved in an infinite regress
in which what exists now is purely a function of what existed
formerly which in turn is a function of what existed the period
before that, and so forth. Without at least a description of the
functional relationships governing the transition from period to
period, we have no real explanation.

I have one final comment about the theory of institutions,
which, while it does not relate directly to Samuels's theory, is
certainly not answered by it. We are told, by economists from
Stigler on, that the function of government regulation is to stabilize cartels. One interesting question is why government is needed
to perform this function in some areas but not in others. Why, for
example, do cartels have to be stabilized by government in transportation but not in the production of transportation equipment
(automobiles)? Is there something about the industries in which
regulation exists which suggests that cartels in them should be
particularly unstable, or particularly susceptible to having
stability produced by government intervention? I don't know the
answers to these questions, but some research directed toward dis-
covering them might be useful.

                              CONCLUSION

As I mentioned at the outset, I feel somewhat diffident in offering criticisms of Samuels's theory, because I really know of no
significantly better theory, or one with much more content. I have
already mentioned the rudiments of the economic theory of politics
which follows from Downs, Buchanan, Tullock, and others. Where
might an economist look for a theory of political power or a model
of governmental behavior? Not, from my cursory investigation, to
political science, in which the technique of applying labels to
the unknown is even more prevalent than in economics. Perhaps what
needs to be done in order to construct a reasonable theory, at
this point, is to provide relatively more empirical input, relatively more specific studies, and more description of the operation of power in specific instances. That means that analysis of

regulated industries should be much less interested in whether economies of scale exist or whether prices are equal to marginal cost, and much more interested in who gains and who loses from specific exercises of regulatory power, and why those particular exercises were chosen.

I suspect that if we did get this kind of empirical content, it might very easily be inserted into Samuels's general theory, or a theory very much like it. The one additional thing which might be added to Samuels's theory is the notion of positive Pareto optimality. Then we would really have a stew that is both savory and nourishing.

2

Practical Economics of Public Utility Regulation: An Application to Pipelines

Donald A. Murry

Some of the recent arguments concerning economic optimization may appear remote from the problems of regulation.[1] The purpose of this essay is to summarize some of the basic issues concerning optimization of rate of return regulation and relate them to a current regulatory issue, specifically the problem of regulatory rate-making for pipelines during a period of a gas shortage.

1. THE RATE OF RETURN ON RATE BASE CONCEPT

The concept of the traditional rate of return on rate base is straightforward and simple. The following description provides a basis for describing the actual regulatory procedure used for rate-making. Conceptually, it is designed to permit the regulated company to set a rate schedule which will produce the minimal revenues necessary to cover operating expenses, including taxes, and a rate of return on the invested capital necessary to attract and retain this invested capital.

Commonly the revenue requirement is expressed in the following way:

$$R = C + (I-d)r$$

where
- R = revenue requirement,
- C = cost of providing the service of the company, including depreciation expenses and taxes,
- I = total investment in plant and equipment,
- d = accrued depreciation, and
- r = rate of return allowed by the regulatory commission.

Consequently, the expression $(I-d)$ is equal to the rate base upon which the rate of return is to be allowed by the regulatory agency. Theoretically, the rate of return should be set at just the opportunity cost level, or the minimal level sufficient to attract and hold resources in the performance of a regulated firm's service. Typically, after a utility's revenue requirement is established, the company submits a rate structure for commission approval. The rate structure, which is designed to earn the allowed revenues, allocates the revenue burden among classes of customers and individual customers.

Naturally, there are grounds for argument concerning the legitimacy of various costs included as cost of service items, C, in arriving at the revenue requirements in a rate hearing. There are further grounds for argument concerning fact and methodology in setting the value of the plant in service, I, the depreciation treatment, d, and the rate of return calculation, r. However, setting these potential disagreements aside, this essay concentrates on the optimality problem in regulation. That is, assuming that regulatory procedures follow the above scheme in establishing the revenue requirements, the issue here is the practical influence of rate of return regulation on optimal investment and pricing policies, specifically in the pricing of the pipeline transportation of natural gas during a shortage.

2. THE AVERCH-JOHNSON OVERCAPITALIZATION ARGUMENT

Several authors have followed the pioneering efforts of Averch and Johnson[2] in arguing that the rate of return on rate base regulation process itself provides incentives for firms to overcapitalize. The precise meaning of overcapitalization, however, has not been entirely clear. There appear to be multiple interpretations derivable from the so-called Averch-Johnson thesis alone, but, for purposes of this essay, there is at least one dichotomy in these arguments that is useful.[3] The division specifically utilized in this essay is between the position normally attributed to Wellisz[4] (a parallel development), although they have been treated in some cases as though they are the same phenomenon.[5] The former position describes the possible incentives for regulated firms to seek a capital-labor ratio that does not minimize cost at a given output. The second describes a possible tendency for firms to expand their capacity for peak service beyond economically efficient levels because of the potential of balancing peak-load deficits with off-peak sales.

Non-Cost Minimizing Capital-Labor Ratios

The Averch-Johnson thesis is summarized in the following way:

> If the rate of return allowed by the regulatory agency is greater than the cost of capital but less than the rate of return that would be enjoyed by the firm were it free to maximize profit without regulatory constraint, then the firm will substitute capital for the other factor of production and operate at an output where cost is not minimized [emphasis added][6].

There are some direct expressions of the Averch-Johnson thesis that follow what appears to have become the conventional meaning of the term in economic literature. Zajac, for example, has

developed the proposition clearly and simply in geometric terms.[7]
The conventional meaning, that rate of return regulation leads to
a less than optimally efficient and a relatively capital-intensive input mix, is the meaning used herein.

Regulation, of course, sets an allowed maximum rate of return;
the A-J thesis stipulates that this allowed rate of return functions as a constantly enforced constraint on profits.[8] In this
conceptualization the product of the rate base and the difference
of the allowed rate of return and the cost of capital equals the
achievable profits under the constraint. Since this concept assumes
that the allowed rate of return and the costs of capital are
constant, it follows that the amount of allowed total profits is
a function of the size of the rate base. Consequently, the A-J
thesis associates larger allowed profits with larger rate bases.
And then profit maximizing management will choose capital-intensive technology. That is, management would tend to substitute
capital for labor, thus augmenting the rate base in order to
achieve a larger total profit. It follows conceptually that, at
every level of a regulated utility's service, there is a more
capital-intensive mix of inputs than the cost minimizing mix of
inputs that produces a higher allowed rate of return. Of course,
the cost minimizing mixes of inputs describe the efficiency
locus of expansion of a utility; consequently, the A-J thesis
argues that under rate of return regulation utilities will expand service along a path of higher unit costs than the most efficient path.[9]

The Practical Consideration

The practical application of the Averch-Johnson thesis, as
stated herein, leaves much to be desired as a source of useful
theory to regulators and the regulated. Probably most important,
the Averch-Johnson influence may be limited severely by the presence of regulatory lag.[10] That is, the constraint, as described a-
bove, must be instantaneously effective and it must be ever-pres-
ent.

Of course, the regulatory process does not function with such
efficacy. And if regulatory actions do not instantaneously follow
when a firm's profit exceeds the allowed rate of return, there
are incentives for management to seek higher profits, under the
present rate structure, by reducing costs. Of course, available
means of reducing costs include seeking an optimal, cost minimizing mix of inputs; therefore, this incentive of regulatory lag
would encourage the firm to operate on the efficiency locus.

Although many authors have considered the regulatory lag as a
countering influence to the Averch-Johnson incentives, they probably have underrated the complexities of the regulatory agency's
and management's relationships.[11] In practice, the management of
a regulated utility is faced with a very complex set of problems
if it sets out to evaluate the future effects of rate of return
regulation upon potentially invested capital versus the loss of
potential profits by not choosing the most efficient mix of inputs.

In taking advantage of the alleged A-J effect, the utility management would in practice, have, at the very best, a difficult chore. If management of a regulated utility is to choose between operating with the most efficient, cost minimizing capital-labor ratio or an overcapitalized capital-labor ratio because of future rate of return on rate base decisions, it must choose between the discounted values of the addition to profits of the two alternatives Among items to be taken into account in management's decision must be the length of time until the next rate case under both alternatives and the criteria which would trigger that case, whether elicited by the company or by the regulators, the actual investment alternatives available to the firm and the rates of the new investment, the depreciation rates of the rate base alternatives, the capital cost variations, the anticipated rate of return resulting from the next rate of return decision, and the tax effects of the depreciation rates from alternative investments. An Averch-Johnson influence undoubtedly exists, but to use it as a description of the motivation of management is obviously inadequate. The resulting choices of management are not at all certain; that is the only practical conclusion one can reach given the imperfection of regulation and the complexities of management's choice.

Regulators in trying to discern whether or not a utility is operating with a minimum cost mix of inputs or a capital-intensive mix have at least an equally difficult, and of course, in practice unfeasible, chore. Regulators necessarily would require the same powers of calculation and they would operate from outside a company and interject that kind of evaluation of alternative technologies into regulatory proceedings as well. With the complexity of types of equipment choices, and the multitude of trade-offs involved, there is little likelihood that regulators could evaluate convincingly the technology choices in terms of their capital-labor ratios in a reasonable manner.

Not surprisingly, because of the complexities of the choice between the efficiency locus and the maximum constrained profit locus, there has been no empirical measurement, to date, showing whether regulated firms do indeed overcapitalize in this Averch-Johnson manner or whether they forego that temptation and choose cost minimizing capital labor ratios. It is not surprising that this type of overcapitalization is not a viable issue in regulatory proceedings--at least until some verification and measurement can be placed on it.

Consequently, the A-J thesis as presented here is not useful in evaluating the investment tendencies of pipelines or the influence of shortages on pricing or investment decisions.

3.   THE WELLISZ OVERCAPACITY ARGUMENT

Contrary to the above A-J argument, there is a more plausible argument concerning rate of return on rate base regulation and

its influence on firms to expand to a level of output exceeding
the socially optimum. This argument is the one presented by
Wellisz.[12] The Wellisz argument specifically concerns the allocation of transportation costs of pipelines between the peak customers and the off-peak customers. Figure 1 illustrates the
argument where DD is the demand function for peak gas, and CC'
is the cost of adding additional pipeline capacity. Marginal cost

1.

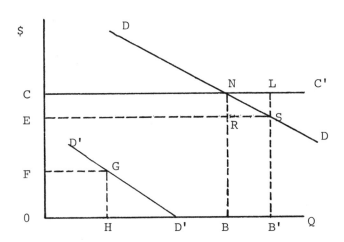

pricing, i.e., P = MC, would produce a peak load price for transportation of OC, a peak load consumption and peak capacity of OB,
and off-peak consumption of OD' and an off-peak price for the transportation facilities of zero.[13] Of course, the cost of service of
purchased gas would be added to the transportation price to determine the final price of gas to customers.

Following Wellisz's argument the presence of rate of return on
rate base regulation will induce the firm to expand capacity to
OB'. The firm has the incentive to expand capacity so long as the
additional capacity yields returns greater than or equal to the
allowed rate of return, and the off-peak price exceeds opportunity
cost.

> It is therefore in the interest of the regulated
> company to encourage peak-load sales through a low
> peak-load rates policy. It will be to the company's
> advantage to push peak-load investment beyond the
> point at which the "fair return" from peak-load
> sales can be earned, provided the deficit on the
> peak-load sales can be balanced by the profits from
> the off-peak sales.[14]

That is, although a regulated pipeline cannot increase its allowed

rate of return through its own action, it can increase its total
profit earned by increasing its capacity beyond B to B' with a
peak price of OE and offsetting the loss on the incremental units
with a discriminatory price in the off-peak period of OF. The
monopoly-like off-peak profits of OFGH offset the marginal losses
to the pipeline of ECLS. Consequently, the total profit to the
firm is now greater because, along with the larger output, the
investment is greater, although the rate of return has remained
unchanged.[14]

4.   THE SEABOARD FORMULA, OVERCAPACITY AND STORAGE

Following the preceding argument, the so-called Seaboard Formula--
as a means for classifying the production costs (both fixed costs
and variable costs) into two categories (either demand or commodity costs) and allocating the costs for ultimate customer billing--
affects the incentives for adding capacity by the pipeline. The
fixed costs, e.g., tax and interest payments, are associated with
the capacity of the pipeline and will remain constant regardless
of the volume of transported gas. Variable costs, e.g., the cost of
purchased gas and compression fuel expense, change with volumes
transmitted.

In developing the charges to the customers, costs allocated to
commodity charges are allocated in proportion to annual volumes;
the costs allocated to demand charges are allocated in proportion
to the volumes of gas taken during peak periods. The Seaboard
Formula, by allocating 50 percent of the fixed costs to the commodity charges and 50 percent to the demand charges, raises the
commodity component to an amount greater than the marginal costs.
Conversely, it decreases the demand component of the customer
charges to an amount less than the marginal costs.

The connection of the Seaboard Formula with the tendency of
rate of return regulation to lead to overcapacity is then a
straight forward one. Since the formula allocates fixed costs to
the commodity charge which is allocated on a volumetric basis, the
price off-peak is set higher than the opportunity cost. For
example, the off-peak commodity charge could be set at OF in
figure 1. Of course, rate of return regulation limits the pipeline
to a fixed rate of return on rate base. Consequently, to offset
the company's profit gained from setting the average revenue
greater than opportunity cost during the off-peak, the average
revenues are accordingly set less than opportunity cost for the
peak period. For example, in figure 1, the price should be less
than the marginal cost OC, such as at price OE.

A most important side effect of the Seaboard Formula is that
it discourages storage construction and peak shaving by distribution companies. Since Seaboard decreases the price of peak sales
relative to the price of off-peak sales, the distributors have
less incentive to buy gas during the off-peak, store it, and sell
it at peak prices.

5. THE EFFECTS OF THE GAS SHORTAGE ON
MARGINAL PRICING CONDITIONS

The above discussion, originating nearly a decade ago, naturally presumes that ample gas is available for the optimal volume sales for both the off-peak and the peak periods. The analysis of the influence of Seaboard on a pipeline's capacity, consequently, is limited to the optimization of the pipeline facility, i.e., the transportation facilities. The increase in demand growth for gas, much of it environmentally stimulated, and a decline in the reserve-production ratio has resulted in a "shortage" of gas at prevailing prices; the existence of a shortage means that at the optimal prices, in terms of the long-run marginal cost of pipeline capacity for peak and off-peak service, the pipeline may not have adequate gas to meet the volumes demanded.

The issue in a time of shortage is whether or not the existence of a shortage (when the value of end-use of the marginal units of gas sold exceeds the delivered price of gas) alters the above conclusions concerning the inadequacy of the Seaboard Formula.

Special Attributes of Seaboard During a Shortage

There are arguments concerning the attributes of the Seaboard Formula, or a similar allocation of fixed costs to the charges of the off-peak users during a period of shortage. They should be presented for evaluation. Basically, they consist of two points.

First, the Seaboard Formula puts higher prices on off-peak users and avoids the "free-ride" by interruptible, industrial users. As this argument is applied to a shortage condition, the peak users of gas, gauged by market prices, surely have the highest end-use values and the lower valued end-users should pay at least equal shares of the fixed transportation costs. Seaboard charges the off-peak users higher prices and discourages their gas usage.

Second, the off-peak demand function for natural gas is likely to be more elastic; in some cases, it may be quite elastic, as interruptible industrial customers use the less expensive valley gas as substitutes for other fuels but convert to alternative fuels during peak periods when gas prices are higher. Indeed the FPC has acknowledged the existence of industrial inter-fuel competition in "tilting" the rate structure away from a strict Seaboard allocation.[16] Since the peak users are likely to have inelastic demand functions, the shifting of fixed costs from peak to off-peak charges should result in a net reduction in the gas shortage "short fall." The potential reallocation of gas away from lower valued off-peak uses of gas because of high commodity charges is an appealing result of a Seaboard-like formula during a shortage period.

Obviously, however, in addition to these short-run market effects of Seaboard, the long-run pricing of the pipeline and related allocation problems must be considered as well, even during a period of shortage.

The Special Attributes of Marginal Cost Pricing
During a Shortage

There are several long-run attributes of marginal cost pricing
even during a shortage period. First, pricing pipeline transportation equal to its long-run opportunity cost encourages the construction of storage. The pipelines can balance their loads in
two ways, thereby filling the pipeline during the valley periods.
The pipelines can sell to off-peak customers at reduced prices,
as interruptible customers, or they can build storage for serving
peak period customers and use the capacity during the off-peak
periods to inject the gas into storage. The cost of investment of
equivalent deliverable gas volumes at the peak is considerably
less for storage than it is for pipeline capacity; however, the
physical requirements, i.e., the availability of old field and
desirable geological formations, seriously limit the building of
storage.[17] Naturally, the storage facilities can be built by
either distributors or pipelines. Also, pipelines can provide
storage for specific distributors.[18]

Table 1 illustrates the apparent trade-offs by pipelines between industrial sales and storage for load balancing. The companies with potentially high storage daily withdrawal volumes in
nearly every case have lower percentages of industrial sales.[19]
Since the differential between off-peak prices and peak prices
is closer under Seaboard than under marginal cost pricing conditions, Seaboard discourages the purchase of off-peak gas for
storage by distributors. Consequently, pricing the peak and off-
peak gas at the long-run marginal cost would encourage distributors to buy valley gas at lower prices and store it for the peak
seasons. The incentive for distributors to add storage is a most
important advantage to pricing at marginal cost, as opposed to a
Seaboard-type allocation of fixed costs. Furthermore, the addition
of storage furthers the movement to long-run optimal gas allocation. The need of pipeline capacity during the off-peak in order
to put the gas into storage forces the interruptible customer off
the pipeline and improves further the end-use allocation of gas.[20]

Investment in storage facilities by pipelines can be at least
as attractive to pipelines as investment in additional capacity by
including the storage facilities in the rate base. The storage
facilities will be equally substitutable for new pipeline capacity
so long as they are treated equally in the rate of return calculation. Consequently, classifying all of the fixed costs of storage
facilities in the demand charge and allocating them to the peak
customer's charges will lead the pipelines to equate the peak
price and the opportunity cost of gas storage facilities.[21] Of
course, storage is a phenomenon associated with the peak demands;
table 1 shows indices comparing the potential withdrawals with the
actual withdrawals from storage during the 1970-71 three-day peak
that confirm the importance of storage during some systems' peaks.

Second, the increase in the peak price of gas stimulates the
use of peak-shaving alternatives on the part of peak users. If the
true opportunity cost of providing gas is expressed and it is more

economical for peak users to shift to peak shaving alternatives
(such as synthetic gas or liquified natural gas), that is the long-
run optimal allocation of resources.

Third, the pricing of gas at its long-run opportunity cost will
discourage peak consumption. Some peak users, if they are faced
with paying the full capacity costs of their service, will shift
from gas entirely. The alternatives available are alternate fuels,
different types of construction materials, and more heat-efficient
technology. Since much of the peak demand is for heating, the
price response in the short-run would almost surely be relatively
inelastic, but over a long period of time, these adjustments
surely would be greater.

The attributes of setting price equal to long-run opportunity
cost can be summarized as stated above--marginal cost pricing will
prevent pipelines from building more capacity than the optimal
long-run capacity and will encourage alternatives to pipeline
capacity.

A Pricing Policy During a Shortage

In comparing the Seaboard Formula to a marginal cost pricing
scheme under shortage conditions, it becomes obvious that the
short-run effects of Seaboard are attractive, but they occur at the
expense of long-run misallocations. The question of a pricing
policy for a shortage period becomes one of balancing the short-
run versus the long-run effects.

Furthermore, by recognizing that the cause of the gas shortage
is not directly related to the allocation of transportation costs
puts the issue of pricing pipeline service in proper perspective.
The shortage results from an insufficient production of natural
gas in terms of the quantities demanded at the prevailing prices.
Not surprisingly, price changes for transportation cannot produce
a long-run compensating optimal adjustment for a market out of
equilibrium.

A pricing policy which is superior to a Seaboard-like formula
would provide for requirements of the optimal longer run-period
(e.g., limited peak capacity, expanded peak-shaving alternatives
and reallocated gas to highest value end-uses). Since the longer-
run adjustment of pipeline capacity, peak-shaving capacity, and
storage can only come about, most probably, through a marginal
cost pricing policy, the FPC should move toward that policy and
away from Seaboard, despite the presence of a shortage.

The short-run problem associated with low value end-use customers receiving gas supplies during a shortage can more appropriately be treated in a short-run manner; it should not lead
inexorably to long-term misallocation of transportation, storage,
and peak-shaving capacities as well. The FPC can and should
address the end-use allocation of gas through policies that avoid
such misallocation. However, if correct long-run pricing policies
are adopted, these short-term policies may be unnecessary. To that
end the FPC has appropriate power to attack such allocation issues
without altering seriously the optimal capacity incentives.

1. Contribution of Underground Storage Capacity
Deliveries of Natural Gas and Percentage of

Area and Company	Highest Consecutive 3-Day System Peak Total/System Deliveries (Mcf)
Eastern Area	
Columbia Gas System, Inc.	30,165,537
Other	
Consolidated Gas Supply Corp.	12,849,861
Equitable Gas Co.	2,068,830
Iroquois Gas Corp.	2,631,983
North Pennsylvania Gas Co.	521,105
Pennsylvania Gas Co.	757,168
Tennessee Gas PL, (Tenneco)	15,730,414
Texas Eastern Trans. Corp.	11,745,513
Transco. Gas Pipe Line Corp.	12,847,676
United Nat. Gas Co. & The Sylvania Corp.	1,712,010
Midwestern Area	
Cities Service Gas Co.	5,998,967
Kan.-Neb. Nat. Gas Co., Inc.	1,514,596
Michigan Gas Storage Co.	1,947,687
Mich.-Wisc. Pipe Line Co.	11,456,011
Midwestern Gas Trans. Co.	3,099,353
Mississippi River Trans. Corp.	2,919,737
Natural Gas Pipe. Co. of Am.	13,632,129
Northern Natural Gas Co.	8,591,880
Panhandle Eastern Pipeline Co.	8,353,546
Texas Gas Trans. Corp.	7,702,880
Union Light, Heat & Power Co.	N.R.
Western Area	
Colorado Interstate Corp.	3,185,380
Lone Star Gas Co.	6,142,259
Montana Dakota Utilities Co.	944,846
Mountain Fuel Supply Co.	1,420,451
Southern Area	
Arkansas Louisiana Gas Co.	3,697,862
Arkansas Oklahoma Gas Corp.	292,141
United Gas Pipe Line Co.	14,947,374

Sources: (1) Underground Storage of Natural Gas by Interstate Pipeline Companies, December 1971, The Annual Report for Calendar year 1970 and Winter 1970-1971, as transmitted to the Commission in BNG's Memorandum dated December 21, 1971.

and Deliveries to Total System Peak
Pipeline Annual Industrial Sales

Max. Storage Deliverability (Mcf/Day)	P/L Annual Mainline Ind. Sales as % of Total System Annual Sales	3-Day Max. Storage Deliverability as % of 3-Day System Peak Deliveries	Actual Storage Deliveries as % of 3-Day System Peak Deliveries
3,371,000	1.3	33.6	35.44
3,867,840	0.0	90.3	57.73
504,200	0.0	73.2	56.07
376,000	0.0	42.9	30.90
110,000	0.0	63.3	66.06
220,000	0.0	87.3	50.46
750,500	0.0	14.4	13.20
1,216,662	0.0	31.2	20.48
1,045,859	0.4	24.3	26.65
355,000	0.0	62.1	48.76
779,700	32.2	39.0	25.90
86,800	26.4	17.1	N.R.
487,481	0.0	75.0	66.05
1,240,000	0.0	32.4	30.94
N.R.	0.0	N.R.	3.77
275,000	35.6	28.2	21.34
N.R.	13.9	N.R.	25.59
375,337	13.4	13.2	12.43
480,070	7.1	17.1	16.82
460,020	2.1	18.0	8.89
16,130	0.0	N.R.	N.R.
174,050	19.9	16.5	14.33
715,425	22.2	34.8	26.95
175,000	19.5	55.5	N.R.
52,531	0.0	11.1	0.63
156,645	59.8	12.6	8.15
15,529	1.2	15.9	N.R.
1,100,000	37.4	22.2	9.95

Sources (cont'd):   (2) Statistics of Interstate Natural Gas
                        Pipeline Companies, 1970.

N.R.: not reported

One mechanism immediately available to the FPC is its certification power over construction. The construction projects for
storage and pipeline capacity expansion, such as compression additions and looping, must be specifically certified by the FPC
before they can proceed. A more lenient policy, i.e., series of
decisions, on storage vis-a-vis the alternative of pipeline capacity could alone cause pipelines to opt for storage where it is
physically available and economically equivalent to pipe capacity.[22]
During certification proceedings for evaluation, the FPC staff or
interveners can introduce an active consideration of storage as
a viable alternative to proposed additional capacity when it is
in the public interest. Of course, during this shortage period
the proposals for capacity expansion will be less attractive to
pipelines and their financiers, and these proposals will be less
sizable and less frequent than in past years. But that should not
deter storage alternatives where they are possible.

The FPC in the rate of return allowed on rate base, has a
second mechanism available for the immediate problem of allocating gas to higher valued end uses during a shortage. The FPC
has the power to make storage relatively more attractive by
factoring into the determination of the revenue requirements a
higher return on new storage facilities to induce storage construction by pipelines. The basis for such a policy is simple.
In the short run, with limited gas supplies, the higher valued
uses will occur on peak; reallocating gas to service peak demand from off-peak users is in the public interest. Although on
the surface this second alternative appears administratively complicated, many pipelines have separate rate schedules for gas
withdrawn from storage. Adjusting these storage rates to provide
an attractively higher return for peak sales from storage could
lead to both the design of a socially-optimal pipeline storage
system (i.e., the least cost system for the gas volumes delivered)
and a superior end-use allocation of gas. Furthermore, such rate
policies could be altered or removed if deemed unnecessary in
the future.

Such a marginal cost pricing policy that compensates for end-
use values on capacity should lead to the following results: (1)
there would no longer be long-run incentives for pipelines to
expand transmission facilities to overcapacity after allocating
the fixed costs to peak customer's demand charges; (2) there
would be long-run incentives for distributors to build additional
storage facilities; (3) there would be long-run incentives for the
development of peak-shaving alternatives; (4) there would be inducements for the pipelines to develop storage and peak-shaving
capabilities in lieu of pipeline capacity, and the inducements
could be flexible, nonpermanent, and without lasting misallocation;
(5) the final decisions to build storage, peak-shaving capacity
and transmission facilities would rest with the individual pipelines, distributors and customers (helping to avoid rationing),
and these individuals would base their decisions on their evaluation and comparison of the peak and the off-peak prices; and
(6) the resulting prices would reflect and express the end-use

values for gas, and these end-use values will affect the final allocation of gas from low value to high value end uses. In short, the existence of a gas shortage is not justification for inducing the development of a nonoptimal pipeline system.

6. SUMMARY

The Averch-Johnson thesis as narrowly defined above shows little present usefulness in applied rate of return on rate base regulatory decisions. On the other hand, the cross-subsidization by off-peak customers of peak customers via discriminatory pricing of off-peak gas is of more regulatory value and specifically in this case concerning the current problem of pricing pipeline capacity during a gas shortage.

The Wellisz overcapacity argument was applied to the case of pipeline pricing regulation during a gas shortage; it leads to a plausible recommendation for pricing that accounts for optimal pipeline capacity, optimal storage additions, and peak-shaving additions. In the time of a shortage, the allocation of gas according to end-use values becomes a more important policy, but it need not preclude the pricing of pipeline services at their opportunity cost. Direct policies, but ones that are not long lasting, are more appropriate for allocating gas to its highest valued end uses.

COMMENTS by Carl E. Horn

I have no problems with Professor Murry's essay. I feel I must apologize for that. Economists are more noted than theologians for debating fine points and quiddities which can be exhumed from the darker recesses of any scholarly essay. But since I am neither an economist nor a theologian, despite some youthful dalliance in both of those fields, I cannot lose any professional stature. I should like to compliment Professor Murry for a good essay, carefully thought out and modestly presented.

He has effectively dispatched the A-J thesis as lacking usefulness in applied rate of return on rate base proceedings. He has turned his attention to one very specific issue: recommending a pricing policy for natural gas that recognizes the need to optimize storage capacity, peak-shaving, and pipeline capacity—with due regard to long run conditions in the industry. This recommendation presents several implications for regulatory theory and practice which I would like to discuss.

His recommendations seem sensible. My first reaction was

one of envy that things could be so simple in the gas industry.
The product is essentially homogeneous--though there are clearly
qualifications needed based on time-of-day and season-of-the-year
demands--the production function is known and alterations in it
can be more or less discretely evaluated. Alas, such precision is
not possible in the telecommunications industry today. Envy then
gave way to outright admiration as it became clear that his pricing recommendation would coincide with the best of all microeconomic worlds, a long-run marginal cost pricing policy.

Dr. Murry is obviously a scholar of independence and distinc-
tion. His conclusions reinforce my biases--reject the A-J hypothesis as an empty theoretical box and advocate long-run marginal
cost analysis as a powerful tool for proper decision-making. But
the fact that we agree does not mean that all problems have been
solved. Far from it. I infer from Murry's essay that it is by no
means clear that the FPC will adopt his sensible recommendations--
to be more lenient in granting construction authorizations for
storage rather than pipeline capacity and/or to allow a higher
return on new storage facilities. I don't know if the industry
itself would welcome such a policy.

In the field of regulatory policy, as most practitioners know,
the question is not so much one of answering what is the best
course for the future as it is, how did we get to where we are and
how will the past influence the future. The question has particular relevance as you review the history of transportation regulation as practiced by the Interstate Commerce Commission. It also
applies to the FPC and its development of the Atlantic-Seaboard
Formula as well as to the FCC and its enthusiasm for fully allocated cost studies. I think it is always useful to apply the acid
question of a semiprofessional Russian economist who said: "If
you want to see your way through a difficult problem you should
ask who is doing what to whom."

So, in the present context, the question is how did the Seaboard Formula arise and who has championed it. A recent article
by Hans E. Nissel touching on this matter ("Do Across the Board
Rate Increases Yield Reasonable Rates?" Public Utilities Fortnightly, June 8, 1972, pp. 62-68) suggested that the Seaboard
Formula was championed by the FPC staff. It was designed to load
more of the fixed cost on the off-peak user of natural gas (the
industrial customer) and to reduce the cost to the peak user (the
residence heating customer). The formula was revised in 1964 when
the FPC found it necessary to permit lower off-peak rates--thus
tilting the schedule to increase demand charges and lower commodity charges. The FPC said: "The most weighty circumstance [justi-
fying this] was the importance of retaining marginal interruptible
sales that might otherwise be lost to competing fuels." My impression is that the tattered remains of the Seaboard Formula are
still present in FPC staff thinking.

The FPC is also the source of another pricing policy recommendation which, if not elegant, is at least honest. In discussing
the difficulty of allocating common costs for rate making the
commission said:

> When an unrealistic result is reached, the formulae
> for allocations must be changed in order to bring
> about a reasonable result. The allocation methods
> then become a means of supporting a result already
> arrived at rather than a means of arriving at a
> result which was previously unknown. [Re Phillips
> Petroleum Co., 24 FPC 537, 544, 1960]

While we are on the subject of regulatory policy regarding pricing
methods, I would also like to wring my hands in anguish at this
point over the Ingot Molds Case which wonderfully exemplifies the
specious economic reasoning of the ICC and that other great re-
pository of economic insight, the United States Supreme Court.

The traditional adversary confrontation in regulatory proceedings biases those proceedings to short-run solutions of long-
run problems. And regulators seem to be seeking certainty at the
expense of economic rationality. The companies may be just as
anxious as the commission staff for the certainty of a simple
formula. But simple formulas don't solve tough problems. The
quest in regulation should be for long-run policies that properly
motivate managers and regulators to achieve, among other things,
a closer approximation to allocational efficiency. Yet this is not
likely to occur. In general, the regulatory process lends itself
unduly to a search for short-run certainty, not long-run flexibility.

The important issue implicit in Dr. Murry's discussion is how
is national policy formulated for a regulated industry. This is a
practical question of considerable importance. In the case of the
natural gas industry as discussed in this essay, one aspect of it
is the allocation of natural gas to end users. His proposal of
long-run marginal cost pricing is a sensible answer to the question. But it is offered here as a rather novel suggestion. Why is
that so? And if it is a proper policy alternative for the industry,
how will it be discussed, examined and perhaps, ultimately, im-
plemented? Does it not make sense to review such a proposal apart
from a specific rate case? Will writing such a proposal into a
specific rate order have any effect on any but the company under
immediate consideration?

Before concluding, I would like to refer to some practical
economic issues in the telecommunications industry. The question
of a proper pricing policy for telecommunications service is being
actively explored in many dockets before the FCC and in state rate
cases across the country.

The issue of what constitutes a proper rate structure has
recently become one of the more controversial matters in those
cases. This is true for several reasons:

(1) special interest groups are pushing their own interests
    with considerably more force than ever before, and

(2) some competition is now permitted in telecommunications
    and these new competitors (many of whom are unregulated)
    are quite interested in the implications of Bell's pricing

policy as it affects their own pricing strategies.

As a result, Bell companies are gearing up to be more articulate
about their policies.

I cannot speak of any System consensus in the pricing policy
area. But I can expose several of my biases:

(1) long-run marginal costing is the proper starting
point for utility ratemaking,

(2) deviations from such a policy should be explained, and

(3) the rate-making process should not be used to achieve
social income redistribution goals, whether or not such
goals are championed by the state (in the guise of
legislators and/or regulators).

The practical implications of these very general principles are
quite novel--from the standpoint of the "traditional" behavior of
both Bell and regulators. Specifically:

(1) should long distance rates be set on the basis of a
nationwide averaging?

(2) should Directory Assistance service be provided "free"--
i.e., at zero marginal cost?

(3) should coin telephone service be priced below its
relevant costs?

(4) should competition be permitted for the terminal gear
portion of the communications market which may benefit
a few customers yet has the potential to raise the
cost of basic interstate and intrastate services to
all customers? and,

(5) should installation of phone service be provided
below marginal cost?

Profound problems of cost methodology and heterogeneity of service
offerings must be dealt with before we can make much progress in
answering these questions. But we should learn a great deal in the
process. The questions should be answered.

We all know it's easier to ask tough questions than it is to
answer them. But let me leave one more with you:

What objectives do we, as a society, have for regulated
industries, collectively or individually--and how well
does the institution of regulation perform in achieving
them?

In general, I think that Dr. Murry's essay is a step toward reason

and objectivity in one industry. I wish I could be a bit more
hopeful that such an attitude would be evident at the FCC before
too long. Businessmen are by nature optimistic. Who knows, perhaps,
Dr. Murry will turn up at the FCC some day.

3

Investment Characteristics of Common Stocks in Regulated and Unregulated Industries: A Comparative Study

Lawrence Fisher

All investments in the United States are affected by the economic climate that results from the carrying out of government policies.[1] However (at least in "normal" times), most lines of business are relatively free from some important kinds of direct regulation that affect the transportation, public utility, and communications industries. In these regulated industries a governmental body is likely to control entry into the business, the quality of the goods or services that are sold, and the prices that are charged. Moreover, when there is regulation of entry, it may take the form of granting an exclusive franchise that leaves each customer with no right to choose his supplier.

From the investor's point of view, the regulation of price, level of service, and market to be served means that the nature of the risks faced by the firm may be very different from that faced by relatively unregulated companies. However, it is not obvious how much difference the regulation makes in fact. For example, we may recall that in the nineteenth century the railroad displaced the steamboat (which was also a nineteenth-century invention) as a carrier of intercity passengers. In this century the railroad, in turn, has been displaced by the automobile, bus, and airplane. In the future, how much of the actual function of travel will be taken over by things like the Picturephone?

The purpose of this essay is to look at some of the possible effects of regulation as they are reflected in the investment performance of common stocks issued by firms in the two kinds of industry. If the regulators are both fair and wise, the expected rate of return on a regulated stock will be equivalent to that of unregulated industries, when risk is properly taken into account. Initially this point may seem tautological because competitive forces in the stock market will make the expected return to the purchaser of the stock be equivalent to the expected return on an unregulated stock whether the regulators are fair or not. That sort of argument would hold in a world of certainty. However, in section 2 I shall point out that in an uncertain world realized returns are likely to be nearly equal to expected returns if regulation is fair but very unlikely to if regulation is unfair.

The regulated industries considered are transportation

53

(except stockyards and local trucking and warehousing); "utilities"--i.e., electric, gas, and water utilities; and telephone and telegraph communications. Other industries are called non-regulated for this study because they seem to have no more than one of the three types of regulation mentioned above or are barely represented among the firms listed on the New York Stock Exchange (NYSE). The line of reasoning that led to the choice of particular definition of "regulated" used here is presented in section 3.

The period covered is from January 30, 1926, through December 31, 1971, and one-, five-, ten-, and twenty-year subperiods. The data analyzed are investment performance indexes for all common stocks listed on the NYSE and for groups of NYSE stocks. Also examined are estimates of systematic risk--"beta coefficients." Unfortunately the data for the period July 1968 through December 1971 were received by us only the last week of July 1972. Hence the estimates of systematic risk, which were developed by Jules Kamin and me, end with June 1968.[2] The use of indexes based on monthly investment performance to estimate how an investor might have fared over a long period of time, rather than the investigation of relatively long-run behavior of various buy-and-hold portfolios, was also dictated by the time (and other resources) available for computation. The files of data analyzed are discussed further in section 4. Section 5 describes the calculations of the statistics that I report in this essay. The major results, which among other things indicate that average returns on stocks in the regulated industries are astoundingly close to what would be expected on the basis of the theoretically relevant estimates of risk, are presented and discussed in section 6.[3]

2. SOME FRAGMENTS OF A THEORY ABOUT THE RELATIONSHIP BETWEEN REGULATION AND REALIZED RETURNS UNDER UNCERTAINTY

In this section I shall show that, in an uncertain environment, realized returns on utility securities are far more likely to be approximately equal to expected returns if the regulatory authority is "reasonable" than if the authority is "unreasonable".[4] This proposition will be proved for a simplified world. I assume:

(1) Firms raise their capital only through issuing common stock.

(2) The expected rate of return on the investor's alternative investment opportunities is known and is constant.

(3) Fairly accurate short-term forecasts of net earnings as a function of the price of the product or service can be made.

(4) A certain world is one in which both future costs and the

capital required to provide the level of service that
might be demanded are known for the current period and
for all future periods.

(5) An uncertain world is one in which both costs and the
amount of capital required cannot be forecast precisely.

(6) Plant and equipment are durable but not everlasting.

(7) New plant and equipment can be provided instantaneously
without affecting their cost.

(8) Capital invested (i.e., the technology used) is not
affected by the return allowed by the regulator.

(9) It is possible to set price so that the rate of return
on invested capital that is set by the regulatory
authority can be at least approximately achieved in
the short-run.

Definition.--Reasonable regulator: One who sets price (and
resets it at the beginning of each year) so that the expected net
income for the year is precisely equal to the cost of capital--
i.e., he sets prices so that the rate of return on invested capital is equal to the expected rate on equivalently risky investments
in nonregulated industries.

Definition.--Unreasonable regulator: One who sets a rate of
return that differs from the reasonable rate. We shall analyze the
case in which the unreasonableness takes the form of making the
expected net income for each year equal to $(r + u)$ times invested
capital rather than r times invested capital, where r is the
reasonable rate of return.

With the model examined here, we need distinguish between certainty and uncertainty in only two ways. In the case of certainty,
each year's income is known. It and the invested capital are equal
to $(1 + g)$ times the previous year's value. In the uncertain case
invested capital will grow at the rate g_o for a number of years.
Then the rate will change (once and for all) to g_e. For simplicity of computation, the probability distribution of g_e is chosen
so that the expectation of $1/(r - g_e) = 1/(r - g_o)$.

The basic valuation formula for this case of perpetual growth
may be derived from equation (23) of Miller and Modigliani:[5]

$$V(0) = \frac{X(0)(1 - k)}{\rho - k\rho^*} , \qquad (1)$$

where
   $V(0)$ = market value of firm at the beginning of year zero,
   $X(0)$ = expected total earnings in year zero,
      k = ratio of net investment made at the end of a year to
           the year's earnings,
      $\rho = r =$ "cost of capital" or rate at which returns to

security holders are discounted,

$\rho^* = r + u$ = rate of return on invested capital.

In finding the value of the firm, we are interested in things like the ratio of $V(0)$ to the initial amount of invested capital $C(0)$.

In the M & M article $I(0)$, the end of year increment to invested capital, is found as $k\,X(0)$. In our discussion,

$$I(t) = g\,C(t) \quad (t = 0, 1, 2, \ldots). \tag{2}$$

Hence

$$
\begin{aligned}
k &= I(t)/X(t) \\
&= g\,C(t)/X(t) \tag{3} \\
&= g/(r + u).
\end{aligned}
$$

Also

$$X(0) = (r + u)\,C(0). \tag{4}$$

Substituting into equation (1), we obtain

$$V(0) = \frac{(r + u)\,C(0)\,(1 - g/[r + u])}{r - (r + u) \cdot g/(r + u)} \tag{5}$$

or

$$
\begin{aligned}
V(0)/C(0) &= \frac{r + u - g}{r - g} \\
&= 1 + u/(r - g). \tag{6}
\end{aligned}
$$

Equation (6) holds when u, r, and g are all constant through time. If either u or g is a random variable, we may, if the uncertainty does not affect r, substitute the expectation of $\tilde{u}/(r - \tilde{g})$ for $u/(r - g)$. (The tilde [~] indicates a random variable.)

We can use equation (6) to analyze our problem. If regulation is "reasonable," the variable u is zero by definition. Hence, the market value of the firm at the beginning of any year will be equal to its invested capital. With reasonable regulation, therefore, the only effect of uncertainty is to cause the current year's income to differ from the expected value because of the lag between cost changes and the adjustment of prices.

In contrast, when regulation is unreasonable, by definition the variable u will differ from zero. If the regulator is a mere tool of those he is supposed to regulate, then u will consistently be greater than zero. If he is overly zealous in his attempts to protect the public or is consciously trying to expropriate the capital of the firm, the variable u will be less than zero. The effect of imperfections in the regulatory process on the market value of the firm will be in the same direction as the error in the rate of return on capital that is allowed. However, the

magnitude of the effect will depend on the growth rate g. If g
is positive, the effect of u will be enhanced. If g is negative
(i.e., if the firm is shrinking), the effect will be reduced.

Table 1 shows some examples of the effect of a nonzero value
of u. In the table, note that the magnitude of the effect is

1. Effects of Differences between the Expected Return
on Invested Capital (r + u) and the Cost
of Capital (r) on the Ratio of Market
Value to Invested Capital (V/C)
According to Equation (6)

Line No.	Cost of Capital	Return − Cost	Perpetual Rate of Growth	Ratio of Market Value to Capital
	r	u	g	V/C
(1)	(2)	(3)	(4)	(5)
1...	0.10	0.00	0.00	1.00
2...	.10	.00	.04	1.00
3...	.10	.00	.06	1.00
4...	.10	.00	−.02	1.00
5...	.10	.03	.00	1.30
6...	.10	.03	.04	1.50
7...	.10	.03	.06	1.75
8...	.10	.03	−.02	1.25
9...	.10	−.03	.00	0.70
10...	.10	−.03	.04	0.50
11...	.10	−.03	.06	0.25
12...	.10	−.03	−.02	0.75

Independent of the sign of u. Therefore, unless the regulated
company is able to adjust g in response to the regulation of return, it appears that the regulatory authority need not bias its
estimates of the required rate of return.

The particular values of r and g in table 1 were chosen so
as to illustrate the risky case. Suppose that the initially prevailing growth rate g_0 is .04 and that the ending growth rate will
be either .06 or −.02 with equal probability. If g_e = .06, the
reciprocal of (r − g) is 25; if g_e = −.02, the reciprocal is 8 1/3.
The mean of the reciprocals is 16 2/3, which is the same as the
reciprocal of (r − g_0), i.e., of (.10 − .04). Hence, if u = +.03,
the expected value of V/C when g_0 is succeeded by g_e is

$$E(V/C) = 1 + .03(1/.04 + 1/.12)/2$$

$$= 1.50.$$

If g_0 equals .04, the value of V/C that would exist if a return on invested capital of 13 percent per annum were to last indefinitely is also 1.50. However, when the growth rate shifts from g_0 to g_e, the value of the firm will shift by an amount equal to $\pm$ 25 percent of invested capital, which is $\pm$ 16 2/3 percent of the market value of the firm--a substantial shift. However, with uncertainty and fair regulation, little will happen to cause the realized rate of return to differ from the expected rate.

Perhaps the most crucial assumption in our analysis of utilities is assumption 9, that the allowable rate of return on invested capital (r + u) will actually be obtained. Then, if u = 0, the realized rate of return will be nearly equal to r regardless of the magnitude and direction of realized changes in the growth rate g. However, when u differs from zero, unexpected changes in g will cause windfall gains and losses that have the same sign as that of the product of u and the change in g.

Assumption 9 is a reasonable one for utilities, but it is unreasonable for firms in competitive industries under uncertainty --except perhaps in the long run because it is the existence of high or low returns that provides the equilibrating mechanism for shifting resources among competitive firms. Therefore it is reasonable to expect realized rates of return to be nearly equal to expected rates only for those regulated utilities that are allowed rates of return on invested capital that are equal to the cost of capital.

3.   CLASSIFICATION OF INDUSTRIES

The archtypical firm in a regulated industry is one which has the exclusive right to supply a product or service within an area that is so large that a potential customer cannot escape its clutches. But coupled with the right is an obligation on the part of the firm to supply all of the product or service that is demanded of it at a price set by a public regulatory body. In many cases the "firm" is an agency of a federal, state, or local government--in which case data on common stocks listed on the NYSE tell us very little about its performance.

Of course, it is hard to think of any service--even clear air --that has no substitutes or that cannot be provided by the potential customer in an indirect manner. The user can and often does take a number of measures to clean air before he uses it: He uses window screens to keep insects out. He alters the ratio of fast molecules to slow molecules by heating or cooling. He removes water vapor with a dehumidifier or the dehumidifying action of the air conditioner. He may, instead, add water vapor with a humidifier. He can also install an electrostatic filter to remove pollen and

other particulate matter. Because of such alternatives, any firm
selected for the regulated class has characteristics that only
approximate those of the model.

The firms on the NYSE that seem to fit best are ones commonly
called public utilities--electric, gas, water, telephone, and
telegraph companies. For historical reasons at least, we must also
include local public transportation companies and railroads for
the simple reason that, even if they are bankrupt, the creditors
may not be able to shut down operations. Their monopoly power may
have dwindled but the regulation of price and minimum quality
lingers on. The form of regulation of airline and pipeline transportation makes it only logical to include the firms that are in
these industries. On the basis of the Standard Industrial Classifications (SIC) we see that we have included almost all industry
groups from 400 to 499. In the investment-performance data available, firms are classified by Securities and Exchange Commission
(SEC) industry group. The SEC three-digit classes are slightly
broader than the SIC groups, which were designed for "establish-
ments" rather than for firms.[6]

Further consideration within the 400-499 groups was on the
basis of including the group unless I could immediately find a
good reason for excluding it. The groups excluded were 422, "Local
trucking and warehousing;" 474, "Stockyards;" and 483, "Radio and
television broadcasting." I have misgivings about some of the
firms in the 411-419 groups, "Local transportation and parking."
From this major group I certainly wanted to include streetcar,
bus, and taxi companies. But I see no obvious reasons for including parking and the rental of cars without drivers. However, it
is difficult to separate them from each other and from rental
with driver and hence from taxis. One reason for the difficulty is
that the Hertz Corporation was once named "Omnibus."

The composition of the industries represented by NYSE regulated firms has changed substantially over the 46-year period considered. For example, in 1926 there were three times as many
railroads as electric, gas, and water companies. However, after
the Public Utility Holding Company Act became effective in the
1940s and for several years afterward, there were about equal
numbers. Now, however, there are three times as many electric, gas,
and water companies as rails listed. Within the transportation
group itself, airlines and pipelines have become substantial--
none were listed in 1926.

Although banks, savings and loan associations, and insurance
companies are subject to substantially more government regulation
than firms in most of the remaining industries, the monopoly aspect of these financial businesses seems to be much weaker than
for typical companies in the utility and transportation groups.
Moreover, for most of the period considered there were few such
firms listed on the NYSE; and the listed banks were all from New
York City. I therefore did not include the listed financial firms
in the regulated group.

4. DATA EXAMINED

The computations reported here were made from two editions of the
CRSP Investment Return File, the 1970 edition (which I compiled)
and a preliminary version of the 1972 edition (which was compiled
according to the same computational algorithms by Interactive Data
Corporation).[7] The CRSP Master File, from which the Return File
is computed, includes data on every common stock listed on the New
York Stock Exchange at any time since the end of January 1926.
Included are each month-end price, each month's volume of trading,
and descriptions of each cash dividend or other capital change in
sufficient detail so that it is possible to trace the market value
of an investment made at the end of any month through the end of
any subsequent month that the original company or one of its
successors in a merger or reorganization is still listed.[8]

The CRSP Investment Return File contains the month-by-month
return on investment of each stock in the Master File. These
returns are computed essentially by the following equation:

$$r_{it} = (P_{it} + D_{it} - P^a_{i,t-1})/P^a_{i,t-1} \qquad (7)$$

where

r_{it} = return on the ith stock in month t,

P_{it} = price of ith stock at the end of month t,

D_{it} = cash dividends paid to the holder of one share of
the ith stock during month t (i.e., if the stock
had an ex-dividend date during the month, the dividend is included),

$P^a_{i,t-1}$ = price of the ith stock at the end of month t - 1,
adjusted for capital changes during month t (the
capital changes that require adjustment are
generally stock dividends, splits, subscription
rights, and the distribution of securities issued
by other companies).

If there are two or more dividends or capital changes, the value
of r_{it} must be described by a computer program rather than by an
equation. (The Return File itself also includes P_{it} and a second
"return" that excludes taxable dividends.) In addition to the
information already described, the files contain the SEC three-
digit industry group or groups for the security throughout the
period it has been listed.

The Return File is much more convenient to pass through the
computer than the Master File. Each file describes the investment
behavior of more than 2,000 stocks over a period of more than 550
months. Since less than 10 percent of the stocks were listed for
the entire 46-year period covered to date, the number of company-
months covered is only about 600,000. On the Return File, a relatively simple format can be used for the data. Each stock's data
begin with a header record which, among other things, shows the
first and most recent names recorded in the Master File, the

industries to which it has belonged (and when), and the time period
covered by the return and price data. The price and return data
follow the header record. Hence a single, although fairly complex,
format describes the file.

In the Master File, however, the arrangement is much more complex. Data are organized chronologically for each stock. There is
a record for each month which reports the price and volume of
trading for the month. There may also be any of a large number of
other records reporting dividends, capital changes, etc. Hence,
the number of records depends on much more than the length of time
the stock was listed. Moreover, the things that need to be recorded in a logical record vary from the dollar volume of trading
in the month, which, if greater than zero, may range from a few
hundred dollars to several billion, through dates, which are con-
veniently treated as six-digit numbers, to alphabetic text that
gives a company name or explains why a particular event was coded
the way it was. In order to keep the record length manageable, it
was necessary to use a variety of formats for the data in the
Master File. Computer programs that use the Master File tend to be
sophisticated and, therefore, generally take a long time to code,
test, and debug.

As a consequence of simplicity of organization, the Return
File receives much more direct use than does the Master File. For
our purposes, time and cost constraints made it necessary to use
the Return File. This was less than ideal because the Return File
omits all information on the history of an investment after the
month that precedes a merger in which the company under consideration disappears.[9]

The returns reported in this study are based on "arithmetic"
indexes of monthly returns to either all common stocks listed on
the NYSE or all NYSE stocks in an industry group. In calculating
an index, each month's data are initially treated separately. The
index's return for a month is simply the arithmetic mean of the
month's returns for the stocks included. Then the returns for the
index are changed to link relatives by adding 1.00 to them. The
index for the end of any month is the product of the link relatives through that month shifted to a base of December 1960 = 100.

The estimates of returns made with these indexes differ from
those shown in Fisher and Lorie for the same primary reason that
the average annual rates of return for periods that are several
years long cannot be inferred precisely from the rates for the
single years included.[10] In these three articles we showed the
results of having bought a portfolio consisting of an equal number
of dollars' worth of each stock listed at the beginning of the
period. Then a buy-and-hold policy was followed as nearly as was
logically possible. In carrying out that policy, cash dividends
were used to buy more of the shares that paid them, etc. Since
investment performance varies among stocks (as do cash dividends)
and since the particular stocks that are listed on the NYSE change
from day to day, the portfolio acquired at any particular date,
even on that date, has a composition that differs from the composition of all the portfolios bought at earlier dates. Hence, the

performance during, say 1961, of the portfolio acquired in December
1960 was different from the performance during 1961 of the portfolio acquired in December 1959.

When rates of return are estimated from indexes of the type
presented here, the estimates for any period longer than a month
are appropriately computed averages of rates for individual months.
However, each month's rate of return is for what is effectively
a "new" portfolio because assigning equal weights to returns for
all of the stocks implies that the composition of the portfolio is
shifted at the end of each month to include all new securities
that came onto the exchange and to equalize investment among the
old securities.[11] In an earlier article I regarded persistent departures of rates of return estimated via an index from rates
estimated via the behavior of buy-and-hold portfolios as bias per
se.[12] It now appears, however, that the differences between the
rates estimated from the type of index used here and the rates
reported in Fisher and Lorie (1964 and 1966)[13] arise primarily
from the fact, which can be regarded as an accident, that the buy-
and-hold portfolios bought before 1940 became dominated by relatively low-risk stocks during the 1940s and remained dominated by
them.[14]

5.   COMPUTATIONS REPORTED

Return on investment will be looked at for the entire period of
nearly forty-six years and for nonoverlapping one, five, ten, and
twenty-year subperiods. For the one-year subperiods we will look
at the annual rate of return that is implied by each of six
indexes: A market index of all common stocks on the NYSE; a nonregulated index of all NYSE stocks not in the regulated index; a
regulated index of stocks in the groups described in section 3;
and transportation, utility, and communications indexes. The
fourth, fifth, and sixth indexes make up the regulated index. The
second and third indexes make up the market index.

For the longer periods we will look at several statistics:
the geometric mean of the link relatives, which can be used directly to find a rate of return compounded periodically; the
arithmetic mean of the link relatives, which is an unbiased estimator of short-run return; the variance of the link relatives; and
descriptions of the regression of the monthly return (link relative minus one) of each index on the return of the "market" and
"nonregulated" indexes as alternatives.

The remainder of this section tells how the tables reported in
the next section were found.

A.   Realized Returns for Each Calendar Year
1926-71

$$r_{jy} = X_{jy}/X_{j,y-1} - 1.00 \tag{8}$$

where

> r_{jy} = realized return on index j for calendar year t (in
>   Table 2, returns are reported as 100 r_{jy} percent),
> X_{jy} = level of index j at the end of year y.

The first value of the index is for January 30, 1926. In order to
make the reported returns for 1926 comparable to the returns for
later years,

$$r_{j,1926} = (X_{j,12/26}/X_{j,1/26})^{12/11} - 1.00. \qquad (9)$$

I have also compared the annual returns of the index with the
return that would have been obtained from a true buy-and-hold
policy.[15] Also shown are annual returns derived from the data
underlying the annual wealth relatives shown in column 16 of
table 13 from the same source. (See note 15.) Since returns based
on the indexes ignore brokerage commissions, the underlying data
were reworked to remove the effect of having taken commissions
into account in that study.

B.   Behavior Over Longer Periods

In looking at behavior over longer periods--five, ten, twenty,
forty, and forty-six years--the behavior of the link relatives of
the indexes was examined. We computed both the arithmetic and geometric means of monthly link relatives for each period under consideration as well as the unbiased estimates of variance of the
link relatives for the period.
   If one is willing to assume that the link relatives are
serially independent drawings from some population of link relatives, then the arithmetic mean is an unbiased estimator of the
population mean. However, even with these assumptions, the arithmetic mean raised to the kth power is a biased estimate of the
(population) mean product of k successive draws. The geometric
mean raised to the kth power is an unbiased estimator of the product of k draws if k is precisely equal to the sample size N (but
is only a single observation since $G^N = X_T/X_{T-N}$) but is biased
downward for k less than N and upward for k greater than N.[16] In
a recent manuscript, Marshall Blume has suggested a nearly unbiased estimator of the expectation of μ^k the product of k link
relatives that depends on only the arithmetic and geometric means:[17]

$$\hat{\mu}^k = \frac{N-k}{N-1}A^k + \frac{k-1}{N-1}G^k \qquad (10)$$

where

> A = arithmetic mean,
> G = geometric mean.

Blume has also worked out what appear to be still less biased

formulas that take variance into account explicitly. Paul Halpern
and I have been working on the sampling properties of still other
estimators that are more time-consuming to compute but are always
unbiased estimators of μ^k.

It must be pointed out, however, that the estimates from the
indexes vary substantially from estimates based on more precise
simulation of buy-and-hold policies. These differences are quite
large for many of the time periods longer than one year. Hence
the arithmetic and geometric means and variance that will be
reported in table 3 must be taken primarily as descriptive statistics for the particular time periods should be made with extreme caution--if at all.

C. Regression Relationships

Table 3 will also report descriptions of the regressions of
monthly returns for each index on the market index and on the
nonregulated index. (Monthly returns are one less than the corresponding link relatives.) The market model[18] and the Capital
Assets Pricing Model[19] imply use of regressions on the market
index. However, in the regression of an index on the market,
the estimated slope will be biased toward unity because, for each
month during 1926-71, regulated firms provided between 12 and 20
percent of the total number of returns used to compute the link
relative for the market. Unfortunately, the index of nonregulated
companies is less than perfectly correlated with the market index.
Hence, as a proxy for a market index, it is subject to random
error. Random error in the independent variable in a regression
causes positive slope coefficients to be biased downward. Our
only "solution" is to show both sets of regressions.

The period in table 3 that should be of most interest is the
entire forty-six year period. When the Center for Research in
Security Prices was established at the beginning of 1960, it was
decided to collect data beginning with January 1926 in order to
have the files start with information from a time that the economy and the stock market could be viewed as having been in a
"normal" state. January 1926 was a full business cycle before
the beginning of the 1928-29 boom in the economy and in the stock
market. Hence, data for periods beginning in 1926 are most likely
to provide "normal" results.

Table 4 will present another set of regression coefficients
of the returns of stocks in the regulated industries on the returns of the market index. These computations were made by Jules
Kamin and me as part of a large study of the appropriate method
of estimating systematic risk.[20] This study is still in progress.
The estimates of beta are made only from data through the dates
reported. They are made by applying the Kalman filter method of
weighted regression. Kalman filters are a generalization of the
more generally known method of exponentially weighted distributed
lags. Estimates of beta are used in this table only if they were
made from at least 28 observations.

Note that the actual indexes, their link relatives, and the

number of stocks used in computing each link relative are shown
in Appendix Tables A-1 through A-18 and that the list of stocks
in the regulated industries included in the 1972 edition of the
Return File is given in Appendix B.

6. RESULTS

Table 2 shows annual returns estimated from each of the indexes.[21] Also shown is the return for the market each year based
on the buy-and-hold portfolio policy used in our previous work.[22]
These returns have been adjusted to remove the effect of the
commission paid at the purchase dates. From table 2 we can see
that returns for both regulated and nonregulated industry
have varied substantially during the forty-six year period. Both
kinds of industries have their values influenced by some common
factors—i.e., they generally move in the same direction. The
general impression one receives is high variability of returns.

Table 3 shows several statistics for the longer periods. We
note that the arithmetic means are always greater than their corresponding geometric means, as the rules of mathematics require.
However, the differences do not seem to be very large. When we
look at the variance of the link relatives (and hence of returns)
we see that, for almost all of the subperiods, transportation was
much less stable not only than other regulated industries (as we
were aware) but also less stable than nonregulated companies as a
group.

Transportation was risky; and it did receive higher returns on
the average, primarily in the last ten years. Utilities and communications both received lower returns than nonregulated firms
and had lower variability of returns. These impressions are con-
firmed by the regression relationships, which show that transportation almost always had a regression coefficient greater than
one while those of utilities and communications were almost always
substantially less than one.

Table 4 shows the estimates of average systematic risk for the
industries that can be found from estimates of beta for the individual firms. The average estimates of beta in table 4 usually are
close to the estimates in table 3. In addition to confirming the
estimates in table 3, the most interesting result in table 4 is the
relationship between the estimated error variance of the utility
betas for 1961, 1966, and 1968 and the corresponding variance
among the betas. Since the figures for variance among the betas
are really for the variance among the estimates, one would expect
to find a smaller value for the error variance than for the variance among the betas. But the reverse is true for these three
cells. This finding suggests that during the last ten or fifteen
years monthly return data have provided no information at all
about differences in systematic risk among utility stocks. This
implication would be drawn even if the two variances were about
equal. Moreover, the results suggest that estimates of beta that

2. Annual returns for one-year holding periods with reinvestment of dividends, 1926-71

Year	Buy-and-Hold	Market	Non Regulated	Regulated	Transportation	Utilities	Communications
1926	-1.1	-2.3	-3.6	3.3	2.7	1.9	12.2
1927	30.7	30.6	29.4	34.5	32.1	42.1	23.7
1928	46.0	43.5	47.6	24.8	16.7	56.4	15.6
1929	-29.8	-32.4	-36.1	-9.4	-17.2	14.3	11.4
1930	-37.6	-37.5	-37.7	-36.5	-42.1	-18.7	-13.9
1931	-47.3	-45.2	-43.8	-53.3	-59.1	-34.2	-40.0
1932	-9.1	12.7	13.3	7.9	9.0	0.7	-9.6
1933	112.5	137.6	145.6	88.6	134.5	-8.3	43.6
1934	15.5	19.0	24.1	-8.6	-5.2	-20.0	-11.9
1935	52.7	59.8	59.0	62.0	47.2	99.2	91.1
1936	49.9	51.8	51.9	48.9	55.2	30.6	22.8
1937	-45.6	-45.8	-45.1	-50.2	-54.2	-38.9	-40.0
1938	32.2	36.3	38.6	20.6	18.9	20.9	11.3
1939	-2.2	3.7	3.8	1.2	-4.8	4.5	26.7
1940	-8.9	-7.4	-5.7	-19.7	-21.0	-20.3	-9.0
1941	-9.1	-8.2	-8.1	-9.4	7.3	-44.5	4.5
1942	33.4	36.8	31.0	77.9	92.1	48.8	29.1
1943	59.2	61.6	56.4	98.4	92.8	115.8	61.1
1944	40.0	40.3	39.9	42.5	58.6	15.7	18.8
1945	61.4	62.5	61.3	69.6	65.3	84.5	32.8
1946	-9.2	-9.9	-8.2	-20.0	-30.4	6.0	-31.6
1947	0.3	-0.3	1.0	-7.7	-4.2	-12.5	-17.6
1948	-2.1	-2.2	-3.7	7.0	7.6	7.1	-7.6
1949	20.8	21.4	20.9	24.3	15.1	37.9	28.9
1950	37.4	37.0	37.1	36.6	68.9	7.1	34.1

2. Annual returns for one-year holding periods with reinvestment of dividends, 1926-71 (cont'd)

Year	Buy-and-Hold	Market	Non Regulated	Regulated	Transportation	Utilities	Communications
1951	16.0	16.1	16.3	14.8	4.6	25.2	11.1
1952	9.9	9.9	7.8	20.3	20.4	20.9	4.8
1953	-2.3	-2.9	-3.2	-1.0	-12.6	9.5	15.4
1954	56.8	56.9	58.7	48.4	73.9	28.0	50.8
1955	20.2	20.2	21.1	16.3	21.5	11.9	14.0
1956	7.6	6.8	7.3	4.6	1.5	7.5	-1.2
1957	-12.7	-14.3	-14.9	-11.3	-30.4	6.5	0.9
1958	59.9	59.6	60.9	53.7	68.2	41.0	77.4
1959	15.9	15.4	17.9	3.8	-0.6	5.6	38.5
1960	-0.8	-1.6	-2.6	3.4	-16.6	21.0	-1.0
1961	29.1	29.2	29.9	25.7	19.1	30.1	31.7
1962	-12.6	-12.8	-15.5	2.4	5.4	0.2	-9.4
1963	19.1	18.9	17.9	24.0	43.5	12.4	18.2
1964	17.6	18.1	16.9	24.8	38.3	16.7	12.3
1965	29.8	28.5	30.8	16.3	40.8	3.6	14.5
1966	N.A.	-7.3	-7.5	-6.3	-7.3	-6.7	-4.5
1967	N.A.	50.0	58.0	13.4	30.6	4.3	8.7
1968	N.A.	29.8	31.8	19.4	26.6	15.6	16.5
1969	N.A.	-20.2	-20.2	-20.5	-32.7	-15.0	-10.3
1970	N.A.	-2.5	-5.4	14.3	4.9	18.7	9.4
1971	N.A.	17.6	18.4	13.4	38.4	3.1	-0.1

Source: "Buy-and-hold," recalculated from data underlying Fisher and Lorie (1970). Each stock's return has been adjusted to remove the effect of brokerage commissions. Other returns, calculated from indexes displayed in Tables A-1 through A-6.

3. Statistics for 5-, 10-, 20-, 40-, and 46-year periods

46-year period 1/26-12/71

	Geo Mean	Mean	Variance	Regression on Market A	B	R SQ	Regression on Non Regulated A	B	R SQ
Market	1.0097	1.0129	.00698				-0.000	1.00	0.996
Non Regulated	1.0098	1.0130	.00695	0.000	1.00	0.996			
Regulated	1.0086	1.0125	.00855	-0.001	1.04	0.879	-0.001	1.01	0.836
Transportation	1.0088	1.0139	.01156	-0.001	1.18	0.839	-0.001	1.15	0.798
Utilities	1.0083	1.0114	.00654	0.001	0.80	0.685	0.001	0.79	0.659
Communications	1.0077	1.0097	.00400	0.002	0.63	0.689	0.001	0.63	0.684

40-year period 12/31-12/71

	Geo Mean	Mean	Variance	Regression on Market A	B	R SQ	Regression on Non Regulated A	B	R SQ
Market	1.0130	1.0160	.00682				-0.000	1.01	0.996
Non Regulated	1.0131	1.0162	.00672	0.000	0.99	0.996			
Regulated	1.0116	1.0155	.00882	-0.002	1.07	0.881	-0.001	1.05	0.837
Transportation	1.0125	1.0179	.01215	-0.002	1.23	0.848	-0.002	1.21	0.808
Utilities	1.0088	1.0117	.00631	-0.001	0.79	0.676	-0.001	0.78	0.648
Communications	1.0091	1.0110	.00411	0.001	0.65	0.697	0.001	0.65	0.696

20-year period 12/31-12/51

	Geo Mean	Mean	Variance	Regression on Market A	B	R SQ	Regression on Non Regulated A	B	R SQ
Market	1.0158	1.0210	.01182				-0.000	1.01	0.996
Non Regulated	1.0160	1.0211	.01147	0.000	0.98	0.996			
Regulated	1.0137	1.0209	.01632	-0.003	1.11	0.893	-0.002	1.10	0.853
Transportation	1.0149	1.0239	.02109	-0.002	1.23	0.849	-0.002	1.22	0.807
Utilities	1.0088	1.0143	.01168	-0.003	0.83	0.701	-0.003	0.83	0.679
Communications	1.0082	1.0113	.00660	-0.002	0.64	0.735	-0.002	0.65	0.738

3. Statistics for 5- , 10- , 20- , 40- , and 46-year periods (cont'd)

20-year period 12/51–12/71

	Geo Mean	Mean	Variance	Regression on Market			Regression on Non Regulated		
				A	B	R SQ	A	B	R SQ
Market	1.0101	1.0110	.00179				0.000	0.96	0.996
Non Regulated	1.0102	1.0112	.00194	-0.000	1.04	0.996			
Regulated	1.0094	1.0101	.00130	0.001	0.79	0.849	0.002	0.73	0.802
Transportation	1.0102	1.0118	.00318	-0.002	1.22	0.833	-0.001	1.15	0.812
Utilities	1.0088	1.0092	.00094	0.003	0.52	0.524	0.004	0.48	0.476
Communications	1.0100	1.0108	.00163	0.003	0.72	0.560	0.003	0.67	0.539

10-year period 12/31–12/41

	Geo Mean	Mean	Variance	Regression on Market			Regression on Non Regulated		
				A	B	R SQ	A	B	R SQ
Market	1.0136	1.0226	.02087				-0.001	1.01	0.997
Non Regulated	1.0146	1.0235	.02034	0.001	0.99	0.997			
Regulated	1.0057	1.0174	.02699	-0.007	1.09	0.922	-0.008	1.09	0.892
Transportation	1.0074	1.0217	.03397	-0.005	1.20	0.887	-0.006	1.19	0.854
Utilities	0.9965	1.0052	.01895	-0.013	0.81	0.727	-0.014	0.81	0.713
Communications	1.0064	1.0114	.01062	-0.003	0.63	0.777	-0.004	0.64	0.777

10-year period 12/41–12/51

	Geo Mean	Mean	Variance	Regression on Market			Regression on Non Regulated		
				A	B	R SQ	A	B	R SQ
Market	1.0180	1.0195	.00287				0.000	1.03	0.990
Non Regulated	1.0174	1.0188	.00269	0.000	0.96	0.990			
Regulated	1.0217	1.0243	.00576	-0.000	1.25	0.780	0.002	1.22	0.690
Transportation	1.0223	1.0261	.00838	-0.002	1.45	0.720	-0.000	1.40	0.631
Utilities	1.0213	1.0233	.00436	0.004	0.99	0.646	0.005	0.98	0.589
Communications	1.0100	1.0113	.00264	-0.003	0.73	0.579	-0.003	0.76	0.594

3. Statistics for 5-, 10-, 20-, 40-, and 46-year periods (cont'd)

10-year period 12/51-12/61

	Geo Mean	Mean	Variance	Regression on Market A	B	R SQ	Regression on Non Regulated A	B	R SQ
Market	1.0123	1.0128	.00109						
Non Regulated	1.0124	1.0130	.00116	-0.000	1.03	0.996	0.000	0.97	0.996
Regulated	1.0115	1.0120	.00090	0.001	0.86	0.889	0.001	0.81	0.848
Transportation	1.0080	1.0090	.00203	-0.007	1.24	0.822	-0.006	1.18	0.794
Utilities	1.0137	1.0139	.00058	0.007	0.54	0.544	0.007	0.51	0.506
Communications	1.0159	1.0166	.00152	0.005	0.89	0.565	0.005	0.86	0.564

10-year period 12/61-12/71

	Geo Mean	Mean	Variance	Regression on Market A	B	R SQ	Regression on Non Regulated A	B	R SQ
Market	1.0080	1.0092	.00250						
Non Regulated	1.0081	1.0094	.00274	-0.000	1.05	0.996	0.000	0.95	0.996
Regulated	1.0073	1.0082	.00171	0.001	0.76	0.832	0.002	0.70	0.784
Transportation	1.0124	1.0146	.00435	0.003	1.22	0.850	0.004	1.15	0.831
Utilities	1.0039	1.0045	.00126	-0.000	0.51	0.521	0.000	0.46	0.468
Communications	1.0041	1.0049	.00169	-0.001	0.63	0.592	-0.001	0.59	0.560

5-year period 12/26-12/31

	Geo Mean	Mean	Variance	Regression on Market A	B	R SQ	Regression on Non Regulated A	B	R SQ
Market	0.9862	0.9908	.00885						
Non Regulated	0.9859	0.9908	.00931	0.000	1.02	0.997	-0.000	0.97	0.997
Regulated	0.9868	0.9906	.00727	-0.002	0.86	0.901	-0.002	0.82	0.868
Transportation	0.9803	0.9843	.00781	-0.008	0.86	0.846	-0.008	0.82	0.810
Utilities	1.0051	1.0101	.00927	0.018	0.90	0.770	0.018	0.87	0.755
Communications	0.9968	0.9986	.00374	0.003	0.53	0.665	0.003	0.51	0.644

3. Statistics for 5-, 10-, 20-, 40-, and 46-year periods (cont'd)

5-year period 12/31-12/36

	Geo Mean	Mean	Variance	Regression on Market			Regression on Non Regulated		
				A	B	R SQ	A	B	R SQ
Market	1.0347	1.0463	.02845				-0.001	1.01	0.997
Non Regulated	1.0360	1.0474	.02792	0.002	0.99	0.997			
Regulated	1.0253	1.0398	.03507	-0.010	1.07	0.922	-0.010	1.06	0.892
Transportation	1.0289	1.0460	.04233	-0.008	1.16	0.897	-0.008	1.15	0.865
Utilities	1.0109	1.0223	.02556	-0.017	0.84	0.786	-0.017	0.84	0.768
Communications	1.0166	1.0227	.01375	-0.006	0.61	0.777	-0.007	0.62	0.776

5-year period 12/36-12/41

	Geo Mean	Mean	Variance	Regression on Market			Regression on Non Regulated		
				A	B	R SQ	A	B	R SQ
Market	0.9929	0.9989	.01250				-0.001	1.02	0.997
Non Regulated	0.9937	0.9995	.01194	0.001	0.98	0.997			
Regulated	0.9865	0.9950	.01835	-0.004	1.16	0.922	-0.004	1.17	0.892
Transportation	0.9864	0.9975	.02499	-0.001	1.32	0.874	-0.002	1.33	0.842
Utilities	0.9822	0.9881	.01206	-0.011	0.76	0.596	-0.012	0.77	0.587
Communications	0.9964	1.0000	.00742	0.001	0.68	0.778	0.000	0.70	0.783

5-year period 12/41-12/46

	Geo Mean	Mean	Variance	Regression on Market			Regression on Non Regulated		
				A	B	R SQ	A	B	R SQ
Market	1.0255	1.0273	.00361				0.000	1.05	0.986
Non Regulated	1.0244	1.0260	.00324	0.000	0.94	0.986			
Regulated	1.0325	1.0366	.00922	-0.002	1.41	0.774	0.001	1.38	0.669
Transportation	1.0324	1.0379	.01267	-0.005	1.56	0.696	-0.002	1.52	0.589
Utilities	1.0336	1.0369	.00721	0.005	1.18	0.697	0.006	1.19	0.637
Communications	1.0136	1.0149	.00266	-0.003	0.65	0.566	-0.003	0.69	0.583

3. Statistics for 5-, 10-, 20-, 40-, and 46-year periods (cont'd)

5-year period 12/46–12/51

	Geo Mean	Mean	Variance	Regression on Market A	B	R SQ	Regression on Non Regulated A	B	R SQ
Market	1.0106	1.0116	.00205				0.000	0.99	0.997
Non Regulated	1.0105	1.0115	.00208	-0.000	1.01	0.997			
Regulated	1.0110	1.0120	.00209	0.001	0.96	0.905	0.001	0.94	0.870
Transportation	1.0124	1.0143	.00394	-0.000	1.25	0.808	0.000	1.21	0.772
Utilities	1.0092	1.0098	.00120	0.003	0.61	0.636	0.003	0.60	0.618
Communications	1.0064	1.0076	.00264	-0.003	0.90	0.622	-0.003	0.89	0.623

5-year period 12/51–12/56

	Geo Mean	Mean	Variance	Regression on Market A	B	R SQ	Regression on Non Regulated A	B	R SQ
Market	1.0128	1.0133	.00094				0.000	0.98	0.997
Non Regulated	1.0128	1.0133	.00099	-0.000	1.02	0.997			
Regulated	1.0128	1.0132	.00083	0.001	0.90	0.916	0.002	0.86	0.883
Transportation	1.0137	1.0145	.00187	-0.002	1.27	0.817	-0.002	1.22	0.786
Utilities	1.0119	1.0122	.00047	0.005	0.57	0.646	0.005	0.55	0.625
Communications	1.0121	1.0126	.00100	0.002	0.76	0.553	0.003	0.74	0.538

5-year period 12/56–12/61

	Geo Mean	Mean	Variance	Regression on Market A	B	R SQ	Regression on Non Regulated A	B	R SQ
Market	1.0117	1.0123	.00125				0.000	0.96	0.996
Non Regulated	1.0119	1.0126	.00134	-0.000	1.03	0.996			
Regulated	1.0102	1.0107	.00098	0.001	0.83	0.870	0.001	0.78	0.825
Transportation	1.0024	1.0035	.00215	-0.011	1.21	0.845	-0.011	1.15	0.821
Utilities	1.0154	1.0157	.00069	0.009	0.52	0.484	0.010	0.47	0.436
Communications	1.0198	1.0207	.00203	0.009	0.98	0.597	0.009	0.95	0.601

3. Statistics for 5-, 10-, 20-, 40-, and 46-year periods (cont'd)

5-year period 12/61-12/66

	Geo Mean	Mean	Variance	Regression on Market			Regression on Non Regulated		
				A	B	R SQ	A	B	R SQ
Market	1.0063	1.0072	.00175				0.001	0.97	0.997
Non Regulated	1.0057	1.0067	.00187	−0.001	1.03	0.997			
Regulated	1.0091	1.0098	.00141	0.004	0.84	0.887	0.005	0.79	0.837
Transportation	1.0169	1.0185	.00342	0.009	1.29	0.849	0.010	1.24	0.835
Utilities	1.0040	1.0045	.00103	0.000	0.56	0.540	0.001	0.52	0.494
Communications	1.0046	1.0053	.00157	0.000	0.74	0.612	0.001	0.71	0.591

5-year period 12/66-12/71

	Geo Mean	Mean	Variance	Regression on Market			Regression on Non Regulated		
				A	B	R SQ	A	B	R SQ
Market	1.0097	1.0113	.00327				−0.000	0.95	0.996
Non Regulated	1.0104	1.0122	.00364	0.000	1.05	0.996			
Regulated	1.0056	1.0066	.00204	−0.001	0.71	0.819	−0.001	0.66	0.771
Transportation	1.0080	1.0106	.00533	−0.003	1.19	0.867	−0.003	1.11	0.850
Utilities	1.0038	1.0045	.00151	−0.001	0.49	0.514	−0.001	0.44	0.459
Communications	1.0036	1.0045	.00184	−0.002	0.58	0.594	−0.002	0.53	0.558

4. Estimates of systematic risk derived from betas of individual stocks

	Date								
	12/31	12/36	12/41	12/46	12/51	12/56	12/61	12/66	6/68
Average $\hat{\beta}$									
Market	1.00	.99	.98	.98	1.00	1.00	1.00	1.00	.98
Non Regulated	1.03	.98	.96	.97	1.00	1.02	1.03	1.04	1.05
Regulated	.87	1.03	1.11	1.07	.98	.90	.82	.83	.65
Transportation	.87	1.14	1.26	1.17	1.29	1.25	1.08	1.33	1.12
Utilities	.93	.77	.79	.92	.59	.62	.64	.53	.40
Communications	.52	.57	.59	.74	.87	.79	.91	.73	.54
Variance Among Estimates									
Market	.183	.199	.210	.130	.152	.145	.126	.170	.177
Non Regulated	.187	.198	.198	.111	.121	.134	.121	.146	.150
Regulated	.139	.208	.275	.255	.327	.186	.113	.257	.179
Transportation	.137	.182	.250	.190	.291	.144	.133	.275	.150
Utilities	.151	.175	.149	.355	.090	.034	.021	.018	.018
Communications	.011	.156	.283	.188	.539	.253	.096	.185	.132
Average Error Variance of $\hat{\beta}$									
Market	.039	.055	.030	.056	.067	.072	.084	.084	.072
Non Regulated	.041	.052	.026	.053	.066	.074	.089	.088	.077
Regulated	.029	.075	.061	.073	.075	.058	.058	.065	.049

4. Estimates of systematic risk derived from betas of individual stocks (cont'd)

	Date								
	12/31	12/36	12/41	12/46	12/51	12/56	12/61	12/66	6/68
Average Error Variance of $\hat{\beta}$									
Transportation	.033	.088	.074	.081	.104	.093	.087	.110	.083
Utilities	.020	.045	.034	.064	.039	.031	.038	.037	.032
Communications	.008	.010	.009	.033	.041	.036	.049	.070	.048
Counts									
Market	647	674	755	809	969	995	1,021	1,129	1,096
Non Regulated	549	578	663	705	820	818	847	943	914
Regulated	98	96	92	104	149	177	174	186	182
Transportation	74	70	64	67	82	78	70	66	60
Utilities	21	23	24	32	62	93	100	112	113
Communications	3	3	4	5	5	6	4	8	9

are made by a regression of returns on the market as a whole are
less than completely reliable primarily because of an industry
effect and not because of "firm" effects. Put another way, the
market or single index model of investment performance is very
far from satisfactory for stocks in the electric, gas, and water
industries. At most of the earlier dates, utilities included both
holding and operating companies. The other industry groups reported here are much less homogeneous than the "utility" industry.
For example, for the entire period the communications index includes both American Telephone and Telegraph Company, whose beta
was almost always far less than 1.0, and Western Union, whose
beta was almost always substantially greater than 1.0. Transportation was almost all rails at the start but has become a very
heterogeneous group. Even when almost all the firms were rails,
betas for stocks varied over a wide range--at least partially as
a result of the variety of capital structures that followed reor-
ganizations in bankruptcy.

Have the returns to regulated industries been "commensurate"
with their risks? I think that the data in table 3 for the forty-
six-year period suggest that they have been. For example, the
Capital Assets Pricing Model implies that the monthly rates of
return are conditionally expected to equal the "riskless" rate
when the market rate is equal to the riskless rate. The regressions on the market for the forty-six-year period imply that such
will be the case at returns of .003-.008 for transportation, .003-
.007 for utilities, and .004-.007 for communications. (Ranges are
reported to allow for rounding error in the constant terms.) The
regression equations on the nonregulated index imply similar
ranges: .003-.010, .002-.007, and .001-.004, respectively. The
implicit estimate of the riskless rate, which is of the order of
4 or 5 percent per annum, might seem rather high to a number of
people. However, these regressions are on the basis of total
returns rather than of returns in excess of the (imperfectly
known) riskless rate. Since interest rates have varied from essentially 0 to over 8 percent per annum during the period under consideration, the regressions are slightly misspecified. Such
misspecification will tend to make the estimated intercepts too
high.[23] Hence, the monthly results appear to be in accord with
the Capital Assets Pricing Model when the regression results are
considered. We can also examine the relationship between the mean
return and the regression coefficient as in figure 1. Note the
linear relationship between systematic risk, as measured by the
regression coefficient, and mean return.

This relationship may also be examined for longer periods by
estimating expected return for five-, ten-, and twenty-year holding periods with Blume's formula (equation 10). These estimates
are shown in table 5. The five-year returns are plotted in figure
2. Note that, except for scale on the return axis, the figures
are nearly identical. The same is true of plots for the other
holding periods shown in table 5. However, these estimates are
substantially different from those obtained by averaging wealth
relatives implied by the indexes for successive nonoverlapping

1. Relationship Between Systematic Risk and Monthly Return

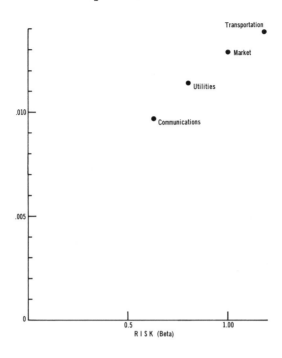

2. Relationship Between Systematic Risk and Estimated Five-Year Return

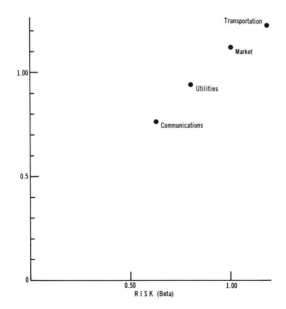

5. Estimates of expected five-, ten-, and twenty-year
    returns on the indexes made by applying equation
    10 to the forty-six-year period in table 3

		Index				
Statistic (1)	Market (2)	Non Regu- lated (3)	Regu- lated (4)	Transpor- tation (5)	Util- ities (6)	Communi- cations (7)
Risk ($\hat{\beta}$)	1.00	1.00	1.04	1.18	0.80	0.63
Monthly Return[a]	.0129	.0130	.0125	.0139	.0114	.0097
Five-year return[a]	1.118	1.131	1.060	1.225	0.939	0.763
Ten-year Return[a]	3.338	3.389	3.084	3.726	2.637	2.039
Twenty- year Return[a]	15.665	16.064	13.541	18.091	10.748	7.474

[a]Return is the wealth relative minus one.

periods. At the present time, the relative efficiency of estimates
made by the two methods is unknown. Hence one would hesitate to
regard the evidence presented as conclusive.

Have I presented all of the evidence that might be gathered
on this point? I don't think so. The method Halpern and I are
investigating shows promise for improving the efficiency of estimates of long-period returns made on the basis of consecutive
observations of short-period returns. Moreover, more precise
results could be obtained from studying the performance of buy-
and-hold portfolios.

Nevertheless, the apparent agreement between the theoretical
and empirical results for average monthly returns of the three
regulated indexes may be an intriguing result for both the
finance and public utility fields.

COMMENTS by James A. Gentry

Professor Fisher has linked components of financial theory and portfolio theory to provide insight into the effects of regulation on the performance of the common stocks of regulated companies. Fisher uses financial theory to define a reasonable and an unreasonable regulator. He hypothesizes the effect of each type of regulation on the market value of regulated firms' equity shares. The CRSP Investment Return File, compiled by Professor Fisher, is used to examine empirically these effects. The essay brings together a clever theoretical linkage and a substantive research design to test for regulation effects. The following observations focus on the assumptions in the analysis and are offered as a basis for productive interaction.

FINANCIAL THEORY

One part of the Fisher analysis depends on the financial theory developed by Miller and Modigliani, i.e., a valuation equation (1) for the case of perpetual growth under conditions of certainty. The original purpose of this equation was to provide interesting theoretical insights to the valuation process under conditions of certainty. Although this simplified certainty framework allows Fisher to establish the two types of regulators, the certainty case is of little value for the decision maker who operates in an uncertain environment. A few reasons are offered to explain this assertion.

First, equation (1) assumes there is no difference between debt and equity in the financing of new investment. In an uncertain environment there is a significant difference, especially the income tax consideration. Both utilities and communication companies are dependent on debt as well as retained earnings to finance investment. In recent years, common stock has not been a major source of funds for these two types of firms.

Fisher's dichotomization of the reasonable and unreasonable regulator assumes the cost of capital (r) and the rate of return on invested capital ($\rho *$) can be defined with certainty. One of the major weaknesses of cost of capital theory is the problem uncertainty causes in determining an accurate measurement of the cost of equity capital. Under conditions of certainty, cost of capital (r) and rate of return on invested capital ($\rho *$) are interesting concepts, but for the decision maker cost of capital is

a subjective concept that is imprecise, unstable, and difficult
to measure. Therefore, in an uncertain environment, it would be
difficult to identify precisely a reasonable or an unreasonable
regulator.

Third, equation (1) assumes the financial objective of the
firm is to maximize the deterministic value of the common stock
shares. If financial decision making is a dynamic process composed
of several variables and occurring under conditions of uncertainty,
is it reasonable to assume we can measure the value of the firm
with four deterministic values? Perhaps there are other more productive approaches to the problem of valuation. James M. Warren
and John P. Shelton in "A Simultaneous Equation Approach to
Financial Planning" (Journal of Finance, December 1971, pp. 1123-
42) have assumed that the goal of the firm is to achieve a growth
of sales objective. They have offered a simultaneous equations
approach to integrate the investment and financing variables and
determine the value of the firm. James A. Gentry and Stephen A.
Pyhrr in their unpublished "Simulation of the Financial Planning
Process: An EPS Growth Model" have assumed that the objective of
the firm is to achieve an expected long-run growth in earnings-
per-share (EPS) and have developed a model that simulates the
investment and financial decision-making process which produces
a distribution of values of the firm.

PORTFOLIO THEORY

William F. Sharpe in the first page of his Portfolio Theory and
Capital Markets (New York: McGraw-Hill, 1970) defines portfolio
theory as the theory of making decisions involving interrelated
outcomes. Professor Fisher uses the risk-return framework of portfolio theory as a tool for evaluating the effects of regulation on
the common stock of regulated companies. The general idea underlying
portfolio theory is that there exists a linear relationship between
return and risk, namely, the greater the risk the higher the return. In the Fisher analysis, if a regulator is reasonable there
is a significant relationship between return and risk among the
regulated and nonregulated industries. If the regulator is unreasonable there is not a significant relationship among the
regulated and nonregulated companies.

In order to evaluate Professor Fisher's approach, the underlying structure of portfolio theory is briefly developed. The
systematic risk measure is defined as the beta coefficient which
is the b coefficient (slope of the line) in a linear equation
when rates of return on a security are regressed against the rates
of return on a single index. It is assumed the single index is a
reasonable proxy of market behavior. Portfolio theory assumes
beta, systematic risk, equals one over the long run. If a security
has a beta > 1, it has greater systematic risk than the market
portfolio because a change in the return of the single index will
produce a greater change in the return of the security. If a secu-

rity has a beta < 1, it is considered less risky than the market
portfolio because a change in the return of the single index will
result in a smaller change in the return on the security. Figure
1 illustrates this concept.

1.

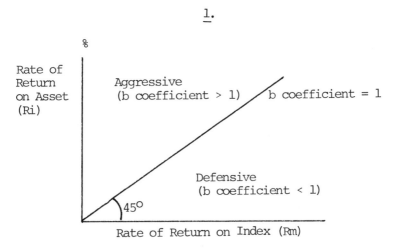

b value = risk. Equation for determining b
            Ri = a + b Rm = C

    Figure 2 illustrates the market opportunity line in portfolio
theory. Systematic risk is plotted on the x axis with the market
portfolio having a beta equal to one. Mean rates of return are
plotted on the y axis. Because it is assumed there is a linear
relationship between return and risk, the market opportunity line
connects two points, the pure rate, on the x axis, and the mean
rate of return on the market portfolio located on the systematic
risk line equal to one. It is assumed the pure rate is relatively
stable and the market opportunity line has an upward slope.
    The mean rate of return is plotted against the risk value (b).
The market opportunity line serves as a decision criteria line for
evaluating investment performance and is analogous to a cost of
capital line. If the point where return and risk intersect is
above the market opportunity line, the security is performing
better than the average investment in the defined market. Alter-
natively, if the intersection point falls below the market opportunity line the security is performing worse than the average
investment in the market.
    The preceding discussion of portfolio theory makes it possible
to expand the dimension of the Fisher analysis. Figure 2 could be
used to plot the return-risk intersections of the various industry
classifications and various securities within an industry. If the
intersection fell on the market opportunity line, regulation
would be considered reasonable. If the intersection fell above
the line, the regulation is unreasonable as the regulator is
behaving as if he is a mere tool of those he is supposed to regu-

late. If the intersection falls below the line, the regulator is
unreasonable and is too restrictive. Thus the size of the differential above or below the market opportunity line is a measure of
the effect of regulation on common stock performance.

<u>2.</u>

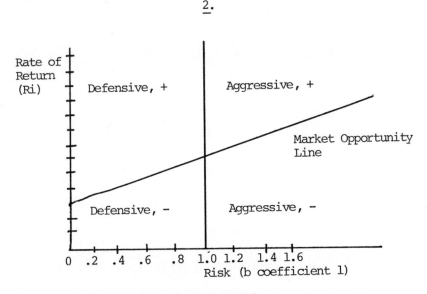

Defensive = b coefficient <1
Aggressive = b coefficient > 1
+ = performance (Ri) > market opportunity line
- = performance (Ri) < market opportunity line

This analysis raises the following questions. Is the instability of the pure rate crucial in the location of the market
opportunity line? What effect does the variability of the pure
rate have on the size of the differential, either above or below
the line? Is the performance of a regulated company's common stock
more a function of management decisions or of regulator decisions?
Does the hypothesized linear relationship between risk and return
approximate real world conditions?

Professor Fisher found a significant positive linear relationship when the forty-six mean returns and beta values of the transportation, utility, communication, and market portfolios were
plotted in his figure 1. The neat fit of the forty-six-year data
suggest that over the long run regulation has been reasonable.
What happens to the positive significant relationships when
shorter time periods are used? Table 1 indicates the instability
of the relationships. These data indicate regulation can be either
reasonable or unreasonable depending on the time period selected.

A major assumption of portfolio theory is that beta is a
stable value over time. Table 2 presents the five-year beta values

1. Time periods when risk-return
    relationship was positive and
    significant, and not significant

Time Periods Positive and Significant Risk-Return Relationship Existed	Time Periods Nonsignificant Risk-Return Relationship Existed
1926-71	1931-41
1931-71	1941-51
	1951-61
1931-51	
	1926-31
1961-71	1931-36
	1936-41
1941-46	1946-51
1961-66	1951-56
	1966-71

2. Beta coefficients* for the transportation,
    utility, and communications companies for
    the period 1926-1971 in five-year
    increments

	Transportation Beta	Utility Beta	Communications Beta
1926-31	0.86	0.90	0.53
1931-36	1.16	0.84	0.61
1936-41	1.32	0.76	0.68
1941-46	1.56	1.18	0.65
1946-51	1.25	0.61	0.90
1951-56	1.27	0.57	0.76
1956-61	1.21	0.52	0.98
1961-66	1.29	0.56	0.74
1966-71	1.19	0.49	0.58

*Betas taken from regression on market index in
 table 3 of the Fisher essay.

for the three regulated industries. Generally the transportation betas are relatively stable. However, the utility and communications betas are somewhat erratic, which could be a result of several factors.

Professor Fisher has written a very provocative essay. As a great researcher, he presents many empirical findings which highlight the frustrations of any theorist trying to find data to support theoretical hypotheses.

4

Public Utility Regulation: Structure and Performance

James W. McKie

The task of the regulatory commission is not an enviable one.[1]
It is called on to intervene in the economic process when the market grossly fails to elicit acceptable economic performance, by
some criterion or other, from some significant sector or organization. It must try to make the performance of the regulated
sector conform to those standards, without completely controlling
the regulated organizations or depriving private managers and
owners of all their rights and prerogatives. The means are often
ineffectual while the ends are not always clear.

The regulatory commission's task becomes even more complex
with the appearance of competition or rivalry in the regulated
sector or on its perimeter. As will be detailed in section 2, competition can occur within the regulated industry, in direct rivalry between two or more utilities, or between dissimilar regulated firms offering substitutes on the market, as well as in a
confrontation of unregulated competitors with either regulated or
unregulated activities of an enterprise whose business extends
from public utility services to unregulated sectors.

In meeting all of the varying problems presented by public
utilities and their markets, regulation has evolved a set of
norms and standards.

1. NORMS AND POLICY STANDARDS

If the regulatory commission intends to enforce performance standards, it must start with norms of some kind. Economists, like
other citizens, would probably agree that the most important norms
guiding public policy are efficiency, progress, equity, and stability or continuity.[2] But these approved norms are not congruent,
and may conflict with each other since different parties having
interests in regulation give them different weights.

If the economist's favorite norm of allocative efficiency were
the only standard, the regulatory problem would no doubt be less
complicated than it actually is, but it still would not be simple.
The regulatory authority would encounter many difficulties in
attempting to simulate the results of perfectly competitive general

equilibrium wherever they did not result from market forces; even
so, that policy would not suffice to meet the other demands on the
regulatory process.

Allocative standards conceal a couple of difficulties, one of
which is defining precisely what is meant by "cost" in the highly
complex activities of some regulated utilities. Another stems
from the fact that allocative efficiency is not attained in one
industry alone but requires economy-wide adherence to optimum
conditions. This is the well-known "second best" problem. Since
regulatory commissions cannot enforce allocative efficiency outside their jurisdictions, the second best standard implies that
relaxation of the rigorous conditions of efficiency within it may
sometimes be good policy if conditions outside so dictate.

The other goals similarly resist precise formulation. One
could say that the optimum rate of technological progress, for
instance, is one which results in marginal social benefits just
equal to the marginal social costs of the resources used in research, development, and innovation. But economics has yet to
discover how to give this proposition empirical content so that
it can support optimum judgments in advance of the decision to
commit resources and guide rational efforts by regulators to control or influence those decisions. The unknown properties of the
social benefits and the overwhelming uncertainties of the social
costs have defied solution. Adding this goal to the goal of allocative efficiency raises some complex questions for economic
regulation.[3]

The norm of equity is an amalgam of value judgments, prescrip-
tive rights, vested interests, and political expediency. Once the
configuration of equitable rights and interests is agreed on (or
enforced), the consequences for regulation can be deduced, but
equity itself is not subject to scientific analysis.

Stability, continuity, and responsibility in particular regulated industries and markets might well be considered as aspects
of allocative efficiency: they are dimensions or properties of
a service or product over time. But this approach can lead to very
complex definitions of the product. It is more convenient for our
purposes to define stability and continuity as separate goals of
economic performance since the government sometimes regulates
markets to promote these ends alone without directly controlling
other aspects of allocative efficiency.

Conflicts among these various norms often appear. From the
standpoint of public utility regulators the most troublesome conflict is between allocative efficiency (implying economically
optimum costs and market prices) and equity (as seen from the
point of view of parties adversely affected by achievement of
allocative efficiency). There are others. Nevertheless, it is
possible to deduce some broad standards for public utility regulation from the various policy norms.

Allocative efficiency implies several performance tests of
the regulated enterprise.

(1) The firm should conduct its business efficiently--at minimum cost, without using resources unnecessarily or in uneconomical

combinations.

(2) The resources committed to the enterprise should earn only a "necessary" return--one which would enable an enterprise in a competitive situation to survive and to meet the demands on it.

(3) Individual prices for services and goods sold by the firm should not be less than the marginal (incremental) costs of producing them. (Some economists would say: should be equal to the short-run marginal costs of providing them.)[4]

Progressiveness yields these standards:

(1) Technological progress to reduce costs should take full advantage of the opportunities afforded by the underlying rate of scientific advance.

(2) Technical and marketing innovations (new products, new services, new ways of providing old services) should appear on the market in a timely manner without artifical restrictions.

The question for regulation here is: how much progressiveness will result from ordinary market pressures on the enterprise, and how much should the regulatory process itself elicit, and by what means? Need public policy go beyond setting a favorable general climate of incentives for innovation, or resort to compulsion on the regulated firm--assuming that means of compulsion are available?

Equity implies "fair" treatment of customers.

(1) People in similar circumstances must be treated similarly. This principle puts constraints on the kinds and degrees of discrimination that a regulated firm can practice if it has the power to do so. The principle, primarily one of law and politics, is no less compelling than the economic principles of regulation.

(2) Discrimination in prices, e.g., in utility rates, should not increase inequality unduly in the distribution of income. This principle can have an effect, though a weak one, on differential prices among groups of buyers.

(3) Long-accustomed relationships should not be upset for ephemeral reasons, and any changes should take place slowly enough to give buyers time to prepare for them. This rule, like the other equitable principles, may result in a deviation from strictly optimal efficiency in resource allocation, or from "rational" methods of pricing.

(4) Equitable rights of access to the market should not be infringed upon for any but the most compelling reasons of efficiency. The burden of proof of natural monopoly in any activity that the utility wishes to undertake exclusively must be sustained by demonstrable facts.

Stability and continuity in the regulation of single industries imply:

(1) When a regulated firm is a public utility offering the only available service, it must stand ready to serve all customers to the limit of its ability to do so.

(2) Service should meet minimum standards of reliability, and the supplying firm must guarantee its continuity within reasonable limits.

Government intervention in the private sector of the economy

is not without cost. Not every failure or imperfection of performance, even of a public utility, cries out for correction--only
those for which the government has policy instruments which
promise a good chance of success. One trouble with a theoretical
approach which visualizes government control as a means of attain-
ing an ideal allocation of resources is that it is likely to mis-
construe the probable effects of control by actual governments
in the real world. Economists may recommend government policy and
regulatory action without taking into account the imperfections
and costs that result. All too often "government" is merely a
code word for the economist's own inner vision of perfection
having no relation to flesh-and-blood legislators, regulators,
and civil servants, nor with the actual organizations, institutional forms, and laws that must guide public policy in concrete
applications. Economics does have a responsibility for systemati-
cally formulating ideally efficient models as guides for public
policy, but it cannot assume that economic organization is per-
fectible beyond the constraints imposed by imperfect institutions.
The boundaries of effective regulation are influenced by both
ideals and imperfections.

Once the public authority has decided to regulate for any
reason it is faced with the problem of what to regulate in order
to produce the desired or anticipated improvement in performance
as measured by the norms it has in mind. It must decide where to
stop regulating and to let the market and/or private decision-
making take over. It must predict reactions to its decisions and
attempt to forestall crippling discontinuities between the regulated sector and its unregulated surroundings.[5]

Obviously, the regulatory authority's choice of control strategies will be influenced by the structural situation that it
confronts. It will take a somewhat different approach to a "pure"
public utility or a highly capital-intensive natural monopoly,
than to an industry that mixes monopoly with competition, where
it must consider the relationship between regulated and unregulated organizations along with the means of controlling the regulated ones.

2. COMPETITION AND THE REGULATED SECTOR

"Rivalry" is a better word than "competition" to describe the
contest among utilities; the case usually presents the oligopoly
problem in an extreme form. Marginal costs are very low compared
to average costs. Nonprice competition has little insulating effect. Utilities are tempted to set prices below the very low
short-run marginal costs in the arena where rate rivalry breaks
out, since they can recoup from other, more protected, sectors
of the utility business. The discriminatory rate structure sets
up inviting targets for selective rivalry, while also facilitat-
ing recoupment out of unexploited value of service in protected
markets. Under these circumstances, warfare rather than

equilibrium results from competition.[6] It is hardly surprising
that utilities in a market wracked by warfare have turned to the
regulatory commissions for enforcement of a joint monopoly with
equitable division of customers, markets, and revenues among rival claimants.

Regulation's failure to contrive any useful model for dealing
with rivalry among utilities other than a joint-monopoly-with-
equitable-inefficiencies model is one of the more noteworthy
shortcomings of the contemporary regulatory process. Nor have
regulators received much useful advice from economists on this
matter. Some have seemed to recommend abandonment of regulation
whenever a rival appears in a sector that was formerly a protected sole monopoly without recognizing that some parts of the
regulated firms would probably retain their monopoly position
and without showing them how to reach an equilibrium in a situation of unrestrained oligopolistic rivalry. Others have called
the attention of regulatory agencies to marginal cost (our favorite touchstone), without showing how rivals can adapt a complete system of marginal cost pricing to the other regulatory
requirements--requirements of revenue without subsidy,[7] and of
reasonable discrimination among customer classes when some demand elasticities have been completely broken up by rate warfare.
Since the marginal cost test is also relevant to competition with
nonregulated firms we shall return to it later.

When a regulated utility competes in some manner with unregulated business, the problems presented to regulators resemble those
of competition among utilities in some ways (though perhaps they
are less virulent), while adding some new dimensions. Such problems are most likely to arise for an integrated public utility
which usually encounters competition in some of its activities
and not in others.

The Diversified Public Utility Enterprise

Public policy usually tries to limit direct regulation of
business to the area that actually requires it, i.e., the area
in which the free competitive market fails to produce acceptable
performance. But if the firm is the thing to be regulated, an
integrated diversified firm presents some structural difficulties
when the public authority tries to decide how far regulation
should go.

The integration problem for regulation appears in two principal forms:

(1) Vertical integration, such as that between a regulated
utility and a manufacturing affiliate that supplies some of its
equipment. Vertical integration in the sense of a combination of
successive processes is ubiquitous in business enterprise. There
are no single-activity or single-process firms in the real world,
and all productive enterprises perform successive operations no
matter what they produce. Economies of scale will probably not
inhere equally in all of a firm's activities; nor will there
necessarily be pronounced economies of integration between the

activities that do and those that do not exhibit significant economies of scale. An inquisitive analyst could probably find many
processes within a regulated public utility that could be separated out and disintegrated. Such services or products are frequently also provided in uncontrolled markets. The regulatory
authority, however, is not likely to recognize and identify these
as cases requiring location of a boundary between regulated and
nonregulated sectors unless the activities are large in scope or
have a significant external impact.

(2)   Intermingling of activities which use common facilities
and resources, or which exhibit various kinds of complementary
relationships. Intermingling can extend from the most intricate
technological interdependence to a distant competition among parts
of the firm for capital resources whose cost and availability might
be different to the regulated and nonregulated sectors,[8] or to
sectors regulated by different jurisdictions. The natural reaction
of regulators to the phenomenon is to extend a uniform regulation
to the joint and complementary activities. There may be no alternative, but that solution may not be necessary in all cases.
Technology may not dictate ownership integration of the entire
supply within the corporate boundary of the regulated enterprise.
In such a case independent markets often emerge which competition
can control effectively. Even though utility enterprises may be
among the suppliers, the regulatory authority may choose market
forces rather than regulation to govern those activities.

If certain sectors of the firm are left unregulated, the control authority needs some devices for preventing inflation of
the regulated rate base or of expenses attributed to the regulated activity--and hence improper inflation of prices there--
by improper transfer of costs and revenues within the firm.
Regulation must also restrain the monopoly sectors of the firm
from "subsidizing" other activities, e.g., intentionally or in-
advertently pricing some of its goods and services below marginal
costs, and recouping from inflated revenues within the monopoly
sector. The control authority is also often concerned with the
fate of competitors--unintegrated firms competing with an unregulated affiliate of a utility, for example. It must prevent the
utility from subsidizing its affiliate or favoring it when buying
from or selling to it and in this way extending its protected
monopoly into adjacent markets. If the authority does not find
some means of separation within the firm to confine these effects,
it will probably try to extend regulatory control over them.

If the authority can find a plane of cleavage for dividing
the organization, it may require the firm to deal with itself at
arm's length between separately organized affiliates. Regulation
must police the boundary to prevent surreptitious crossing and
smuggling by night, but at least it has a convenient focus for
doing so. When it does not have a clean interface along which
to divide its sector of regulation from other sectors of the firm,
it can endeavor to construct a workable though artificial division.
One approach is to simulate competitive transfer prices, allocation of capital resources, etc., within the firm by reference to

outside factors such as comparable market prices. Another is to
use cost allocations as a means of dividing the indivisible.
(Government authorities also attempt sporadically to prohibit
certain kinds of integration outright, by statute or rule, especially integration of substitute or competing activities, but
this approach is not uniform nor consistent.)

Economists have scarcely a good word to say for cost allocations of the kind that divide full costs--both variable and
fixed--among activities in proportion to some arbitrary factor such
as relative average use, space occupied by each activity, physical
dimensions of output, etc. Economics prefers the logic of marginal
cost of a single activity or defined sector that jointly uses the
resources of the regulated firm along with other activities that
lie outside the sphere of regulation we are considering. It might
be possible to determine the marginal cost and incremental investment outlay of one such activity by varying it while holding
the others constant, after defining the time period applying to
the pricing decisions and investment decisions in question. In
fact such experiments are hardly ever tried. Regulators determine
incremental investment cost by assumption, or at best by simulation or hypothetical calculation.

When a diversified public utility offers goods or services to
competitive, unregulated markets in addition to those covered by
its utility franchise, the regulatory authority is frequently
driven to consider whether (1) to permit the regulated firm to
continue to serve the competitive market on an unregulated basis,
or (2) to regulate all of the firm's activities notwithstanding
its participation in some competitive markets, or (3) to attempt
to extend control over the presently unregulated market, or (4)
to force the utility to disintegrate and divest itself of the
nonregulated activities. If it chooses (1), the control authority
is again faced with the boundary problem: the criteria for pricing and the allocation of investment for rate-of-return control.
The firm's activities on both sides of the boundary will be
affected by these decisions. The problems of intermingling of
regulated and nonregulated activities are well illustrated in the
developing field of data communications.

An Example: Data Communications

The development of automatic data processing has created a new
industry which is closely related to communications and in part
intermeshed with it. Development of communications links to transmit data directly to, from, and between computers began early in
the computer age growing out of the simpler forms of data communication in the age of electromechanical data processing.

Data communications have appeared in many forms. Private-line
systems use wire, microwave, or satellite channels in either a
time-sharing or a batch-processing mode. A few data-processing
systems operate with their own communications, especially over
short distances on the premises of the operator: but most use
leased facilities that are at least temporarily dedicated to the

use of that system. Regulated common carriers supplying private
lines that serve different organizations usually require that
information transmitted over the lines relate to the joint business of the organizations. (This is the "authorized user" condition of the common carrier's tariff.) In public exchange systems,
computers, other central distributors and receivers of information,
and terminals make connection intermittently through the public
switched (exchange) network, and are connected only while the
communication lasts. It makes little difference whether the com-
municating parties are members of the same organization as long
as each has equipment that can utilize the common carrier network.

The elements in data communications systems that best illustrate the intermingling of data processing and transmission are
line or circuit switching and message switching. These are functions that all general-purpose communications systems must perform
if users (subscribers, terminals, or whatever) are not directly
and continuously connected to each other. Circuit switching is
a means of connecting users of the network directly with each
other so that they can use it simultaneously--either in two-way
conversational mode or in one-way transmission. Circuit switching
devices range from the old-fashioned telephone switchboard through
automatic electrical and electronic switching equipment, culmi-
nating in computer-handled line switching exemplified by the
Electronic Switching System (ESS) of the American Telephone and
Telegraph Company. Message switching is not necessarily simultaneous communication between sender and receiver (though in
practice it may be nearly so) and need not permit interaction or
immediate response from the receiver. The sender's line and the
receiver's line need not be open simultaneously for transmission.
The messages come in to a central point or point of transfer,
are usually stored for varying lengths of time, are switched onto
the receiver's line and forwarded. Of course the process may require several switching centers and several forwarding operations.

In the 1960s, computers began to replace the electromechanical
systems of message switching, storing, and forwarding used earlier,
such as the "torn tape" method used in teletype networks. Most
digital computers can be adapted for either or both functions:
data processing and message switching. Once a "message" consisting
of data, heading, and address has been translated to machine-
sensible form, it can be processed (transformed) en route while
the system is storing and forwarding it.[9] Furthermore, the dis-
tinction between line (circuit) switching and message switching
tends to break down in computer-equipped systems operating in a
real-time or time-sharing mode, since message switching can be
practically instantaneous (even when it includes some processing)
and two-way communication is possible. The computer thus has
blurred the dividing lines that used to exist between communication and processing information, and between switching circuits
and carrying messages. It consequently has created some stress
for a regulatory system that substantially demarcates its sphere
of regulation by identifying "communications."[10]

Problems for Regulation Created by Intermixing

The intermixing of data processing and communications complicates
regulation in the following ways; they are indicative of the problems regulators are likely to face in any industry mingling regulated and unregulated activities:

1.   Data processors, who are not regulated, can transmit a
variety of "messages" (whether strictly in the form of "data" or
not) over the channels they lease from the common carriers or over
those that they install themselves to connect with other organizations. The messages often consist of processed information. Processors can collect and transform data practically while transmitting it. This capability tempts data processors to become
something like common carriers themselves, i.e., to enter the sale
market for communications services. It also presents the question
of whether such a system may have rights of connection with the
common carrier network. The issue is similar to the one that any
user of leased facilities might pose if he begins to transmit
messages for others. (The "authorized user" provision of common
carrier tariffs is designed to restrain that in the interests of
the carriers.) But the technical capacity of a computer-controlled
communications channel to gather, transform, transmit, and switch
information in a data network is vastly greater than that, for
example, of a weather advisory service using leased telephone
lines. The technology of data communications in a digital transmission mode[11] is itself new with a still unrealized potential.
Control of a vital new field of commercial communications is at
stake. Its relation to common-carrier regulation is still in
doubt.

2.   Even when they wish only to transmit their own data and do
not intend to carry information for others, data processors may
find it worth the cost to enter with communications facilities of
their own rather than to use the facilities of the common carrier.
When the regulated common carrier does not currently offer digital
transmission, other firms--either affiliates of the data processors or third parties--have a strong motive to enter both private
and common carriage of digital communications if the regulatory
authority permits. Entry affects either actual or potential markets of the existing utilities--often very lucrative ones.

3.   Firms offering communications facilities for hire, under
regulation, can also process data, using the excess capacity of
some types of computers used at other times for message and line
switching. These firms may also find economies, or at least advantages, of unified operation of communications channels with the
terminals and computers using them, in which event the thrust of
their business expansion will tend to follow the route of integration of data processing with transmission.[12]

4.   To the extent that data processors are dependent upon
common carriers for communications facilities, they face two
possible dangers:

      a) If the common carrier itself offers data processing to
the market, and has a monopoly of communications service needed

by independent data processors, it is in a position to exert a
classic "integration squeeze" on those competitors--unless regulation prevents it from doing so; how to prevent it is of course the
boundary problem for regulation in this case.

b) Even if the communications supplier does not process
data, it has an interest in how much of the attached equipment--
modems, terminals, computers, and message switching devices--
should belong to it and constitute part of the common carrier
facilities. In many, though not all, instances it has a strong
motive for including as much as possible of this attached equipment under the regulatory tent. Regulators in turn must determine
how far it may go in doing so--another boundary problem.

Thus the growth of communications links among computers has
posed some classical regulatory issues in new forms--entry, cream-
skimming, resale of utility and common carrier services, interconnection, attachments, equal access by customers, tactics of
exclusion by regulated utilities providing services to competitors, transfer prices between regulated and unregulated sectors
of a firm, and standards for pricing the regulated services.

Because message switching in data communication mixes communications and data processing, it has already claimed the attention of regulatory policy. If it is defined as "communication" and
regulated by definition, then unregulated data processors must
either be prohibited from doing it or suffer regulation of part
of their business separated along an undefined boundary. The question has come up in several cases, notably Bunker-Ramo and Aero-
nautical Radio Inc. (ARINC). The attempt of Bunker-Ramo in 1965
to offer a message service to subscribers who were using its
remote-access stock-quotation service was aborted when the common
carriers refused to lease lines to it, on the ground that Bunker-
Ramo itself would be entering common-carrier communications.[13]
(Bunker-Ramo did not attempt to build its own communications net
as an alternative.) On the other hand, ARINC, which provided record
information to airlines on weather, traffic, and reservations,
had also been permitted to switch and forward messages for its
customers relating to these matters. Message switching was held
to be incidental to the main purpose of the information processing network; ARINC was not transmitting common-carreer communications for hire.[14]

The line is a thin one. The present policy on message switching seems to be this: firms may do message switching and forwarding internally, with their own facilities or on lines leased from
common carriers, but they may not do it for others even with
their own facilities unless it is incidental to the main purposes
of processing and transmitting data or special information--a
specialized purpose in a specialized network.

3. COMPETITIVE ENTRY AND THE REGULATED SECTOR,
ILLUSTRATED BY DATA COMMUNICATIONS

The minimum scope of regulation depends largely on the extent and
locus of economies of scale and of integration. In the regulated
sectors where entry can take place (because of a technological
change in economies of scale and/or integration, or because they
were never very pronounced in that sector in the first place),
will there be further need for regulation? Can the government
simply draw back the frontier of regulation, even though it will
cut across utility firms whose other activities, or some of them,
will continue to be regulated? Most of us would find it easier
to write down the theoretical equilibrium requirements for efficient performance under such conditions than to advise the regulatory commissions how to recognize them in practice, or how to
manage the transition to a completely unregulated market with a
reasonable expectation of optimum performance. The expectation
will vary with the circumstances of industry structure, as usual.
Perhaps a further analysis of our case of data communications
will help to illustrate the problems, though no two cases present
exactly the same ones.

Economies of Scale and of Integration
in Data Communications

The scope of the natural monopoly in the communications sector
depends on geographical form, on density of use of given trunk
lines, and on a certain amount of necessary integration between
line and switching equipment. It appears most strongly in locally
switched wire voice networks. In trunk line communications and
the switching services connecting trunk lines, economies of scale
and integration are less decisive. Different exchange areas can
be under different ownership, and so can private (leased) lines
not requiring switching. Trunk line services under different
ownership and control can duplicate each other on dense routes.[15]
Message switching (store-and-forward) can be furnished economically at trunk line connections and terminals by computers that
are not an integral part of the plant facilities of the communications supplier.

What about terminal equipment? Perhaps there is no need to
recapitulate this argument. The attempt of the common carriers
to monopolize terminal equipment, so long successful for AT&T,
may have suffered irremediable defeat in the Carterfone case.[16]
The principle that always should have prevailed--that terminals
must reasonably protect systemic integrity, rather than that they
must be owned by the carrier--now seems on its way to establish-
ment. As it happens, AT&T never made much of an attempt to control
computers nor computer terminals as such under its rules on terminals, only the conversion devices, pickups and modems. (Even now
it requires attachment of its own modem to a computer attached to
its lines, even though the terminal may come already equipped
with a perfectly serviceable one.) Apart from these, no economies

of integration are claimed and thus regulation of data transmission does not have to include the terminals in the rate base or
supervise their prices--unless, of course, it should happen to
pull the whole of data processing under its control.

The common carriers have shown a strong reluctance to offer
digital facilities, obviously because of diseconomies of integration between digital and analog transmission and because
excess capacity on the existing analog system can be effectively
used for data communication. It is more economical from the point
of view of the carrier to use the capacity this way. Because competitive choices have been lacking, we do not usually know whether
the value of digital services to the data processor would compen-
sate for any excess of the long-run marginal cost of a digital
system over the marginal cost of the existing analog system. However, an opportunity clearly exists for independent communications
suppliers to enter with digital services in large markets, if they
can secure the right to enter and if they can either establish a
large-scale system of their own or secure the right to intercon-
nect with certain parts of the existing common-carrier networks.

If substantial economies of scale in communications show up
primarily in the local wired network[17] and switching elements,
then other sectors (such as private lines that do not require
line switching, microwave and satellite channels, and a separate
dedicated digital system) are eligible for competitive entry.
Those elements could be integrated with data processing by firms
that wish to set up their own exclusive communications links,
without requiring extension of regulation to the integrated unit.

We should also ask whether economies of scale and integration,
of the kind that may force natural monopoly, are likely to arise
on the data processing side of the house. Can communications-
served data processing itself be controlled effectively by the
competitive market?

Evidence is fairly abundant that in the present phase of computer technology economies of scale are not great enough to limit
effective competition except in local markets of a specialized
kind. If anything, data transmission facilities linking such
markets to larger centers tend to break down these local enclaves
of monopoly.

Will communications-served data processing and information
systems expand to displace stand-alone systems and integrate all
computer applications into a single all-purpose system--the "computer utility"? Or even if a computer utility does not gobble up
the stand-alone systems, will the computers served by communications eventually become integrated in a monopoly network, to
which neither independent suppliers of communications nor independent suppliers of data processing services can have access?
If so, it would be a prime candidate for utility regulation.

Present opinion, even among the optimists on time-sharing, is
generally against these eventualities. The potential capacity of
the hardware itself, as seen from the present time, is not decisive one way or the other, but the primary obstacle to the "data
utility" or to any comprehensive all-purpose time-shared system,

is the software. The tendency for software problems to proliferate
as time-shared systems become more complex and include more users
has often been remarked. Larger hardware capacity does not offset
the control and program diseconomies if it is accompanied by increased complexity; the latter is very likely to bring self-
paralysis to a time-shared system at a finite point regardless
of the speed of the computer.[18] But it is precisely in the complex
multiple-use system that the threat of natural monopoly has been
discerned. It seems to me that this threat is more likely in
dedicated single-purpose systems served by communications, where
the impact is bound to be much less significant. However, if it
should appear, e.g., that only one airlines reservation service
can exist in the United States because of economies of scale,
perhaps some rules of fair access, fair prices, and mandatory
service would have to be imposed on it by someone (the CAB if not
the FCC) to prevent fee gouging and an integration squeeze. I do
not know whether this outcome is probable, nor can I guess whether
it would use common carrier facilities for communication or set
up its own. Some interesting questions of access by potential
users arise either way.

Competitive Entry Into Data Communications

Several firms have filed applications with the Federal Communications Commission to set up data communications facilities to serve
others, in a specialized mode. The most interesting of these proposals is that of the Data Transmission Company, or DATRAN.

DATRAN proposes a switched digital network, using state-of-
the-art technology, to serve data processing customers in 35 major
metropolitan areas. It promises a higher reliability and faster
connection times than those now available through existing analog
networks. Its system is to include 244 microwave repeater stations,
10 computerized switching stations, and individual circuits within
cities to customer locations. The firm is a subsidiary of University Computing Company, which will be one of its customers, but it
will be operated separately as a common carrier offering a tar-
iffed service to all applicants.

If enough additional competitors enter into various segments
of the communications network, presumably those segments can be
released from regulation to enter the domain of the competitive
market. The number might well vary in different segments of the
end-to-end system. At some points the independent carriers might
be obliged to use the facilities of others, e.g., wired CATV systems for local distribution. Whenever economies of scale did continue to preclude competition in a digital network, full rights
of interconnection with those monopoly segments would be necessary to promote competition in the other segments. This would
present the usual regulatory difficulties: "The problem is to
decide at what price a carrier must offer interconnection to a
potential competitor, as opposed to the price at which it would
happily offer it. What is sought by a mandatory connection rule
is a lower price."[19]

Is a competitive equilibrium likely where entry takes place
in the communications system? Of course oligopoly, rather than a
truly competitive structure, could result. But a more immediate
problem is the reaction of the existing carriers. If several
firms enter digital transmission, AT&T is certain to be one of
them; it is already in the market on a substantial scale, transmitting data over its analog network. (So is Western Union, over
its TWX/TELEX and data networks, but the great difference in the
size and strength of the two carriers inevitably centers our
questions on AT&T.) Naturally, the entrenched common carriers
regard the entry of DATRAN and other firms as "cream skimming,"
even though their own digital facilities are as yet rudimentary.
The entrants no doubt do intend to skim a potentially lucrative
market if not an existing one. The reaction of AT&T is best expressed in its brief:

> It should be understood that the public interest
> would not be served if the Commission imposed any
> restrictions which would preclude the existing carriers
> from providing any competitive services. It should also
> be made clear that all will be allowed to use long-
> run marginal costs as relevant criteria in establishing
> rates, and that departure from nationwide rate struc-
> tures is a most likely consequence of competition. [p. 7]
> [The Commission] should at the outset adopt rules
> for competition equally applicable at all competitors,
> including existing carriers . . . . Moreover, there
> must be no protection of inefficient specialized common
> carriers who have no economic basis for survival.
> The consequence of this competition is clear.
> Existing carriers, including the Bell System, would
> be required to depart from the existing nationwide
> rate structure where that practice inhibits their
> ability to meet competition effectively. [p. 82][20]

These sentiments appear unexceptionable from the point of
view of the economist observer. We welcome competition as a substitute for tight regulation; we think marginal cost is the correct test for price under the criterion of allocative efficiency,
we oppose protecting any firm against competition as long as that
criterion is met. Why then does such a pronouncement by Bell
cause such apprehension among its potential specialized competitors?
Perhaps the episode of Telpak service, which AT&T offered at
discounts of up to 85 percent to meet the competition of private
microwavecarriers and Western Union, will explain some of this
apprehension. It is a question of translating the concepts of
marginal cost and competitive rates into practice, in a context
in which one of the competitors is not only vastly larger and
more powerful than the others but offers multiple services which
are at present regulated under tariffs that leave plenty of room
for recoupment of losses on competitive services from monopoly
revenues on the protected ones. Data communications can be left

to free "competition"[21] only if a workable and secure boundary
within AT&T can be set up, just outside its natural monopoly, to
contain its monopoly power.

Though the marginal cost criterion for pricing data services
should theoretically do that--should prevent "cross-subsidization"
or the improper transfer of revenue from the protected sectors to
those where Bell seeks to "meet" competition--the actual price
that will be equal to marginal cost is not easy to determine.
Bell's rivals, who as yet have no plant at all, and who will offer
a single specialized service, want (and anticipate) prices that
will cover their long-run marginal costs, i.e., their full costs.
Will AT&T costs be less than theirs? Possibly, because of economies of scale and integration. But maybe only its prices will be
lower. The FCC will have to exercise care to verify the former
rather than merely permitting the latter.

4. MARGINAL COST APPLIED TO UTILITY RATES IN A CONTEXT OF COMPETITION

The debate on marginal cost as a criterion for public utility
rates has gone on for so long that one might expect it to have
ironed out all difficulties of principle and application. It has
indeed produced general agreement on the main issue--that marginal
cost rather than average cost is the correct criterion for allocative efficiency. Most economists are probably persuaded of the
theoretical correctness of short-run marginal cost as a basis for
price, and would agree under ideal assumptions that even public
utilities should set prices equal to short-run marginal cost.
But it is another matter to specify marginal cost exactly and to
prescribe application of the criterion to concrete cases.

An extensive analysis of the problem was recently offered by
Alfred Kahn, who is an optimist about the principle if not the
practice:

> The outcome of this entire discussion about the
> problems of defining (as contrasted with actually
> measuring and applying) marginal cost is that neither
> the choice between short and long-run, nor the prob-
> lem of defining the incremental unit of sale, nor the
> prevalence of common and joint costs raises any diffi-
> culties in principle about the economically efficient
> price. It is set at the short-run marginal cost of
> the smallest possible additional unit of sale.[22]

This statement is undoubtedly correct as far as it concerns
the pure logic of marginal cost, though the pure logic tends to
reduce marginal cost to an imponderable quantity. The axioms of
this logic are those of static economic theory. Those axioms, as
everyone knows, do not purport to describe the real world. When
one attempts to specify more completely the relevant facts, the

dimensions of reality from which the various influences on marginal cost must come, to give the concept some form and weight,
is one introducing problems of "measuring and applying" or still
roughing in the "principles" and defining the concept? One never
knows. In any event the realistic definition, measurement, and
application of the concept are unquestionably more puzzling than
the logical role of the concept in static price theory. Kahn
himself notes several problems:

1. Businesses cannot calculate the marginal costs that correspond to the concept.

2. Marginal costs (as defined) vary widely from one moment
to the next.

3. Since excess capacity in the short run is typical, if
firms typically did base prices on short-run marginal cost they
would not cover their full costs, i.e., they would typically go
bankrupt.

4. When common costs are present, as they usually are in
public utilities, prices equal to the separate marginal costs
would likewise typically fail to cover full costs of supply.

5. Prices equal to short-run marginal costs as defined would
probably lead to chaotic market conditions and predatory
competition.[23]

One wonders how a principle subject to reservations like these
can make any claim to be an "ideal" criterion for pricing. Implicit in these reservations is what we might call the problem of
sequence. When a criterion such as marginal cost is proposed for
pricing, business firms (including utilities) that heed it must
make decisions in real time, serially. Economic theory, the logical foundation of the marginal cost principle, does not need to
concern itself with this problem because it is essentially timeless. Markets are without sequence or progression. Production,
demand, and supply are expressed as rates, or quantities per
unit of time when time is arrested and frozen, or when nothing
whatever changes during the relevant period. "The" marginal cost
is the one associated with the assumed output rate, and is the
same for all units of output. In markets without price discrimination, recontracting is continuously possible and encounters no
friction. Buyers can reach the uniform equilibrium price, equal
to marginal cost for the equilibrium rate of output, without
regard to the sequence of decisions and bargains in the market.

In the actual world, if the short-run marginal cost varies
much over time as these short-run "periods" succeed one another,
the ideal price must also vary as it relates to these short-run
periods. Kahn hints at the difficulty in the following illustration:

> Consider the passenger airplane already scheduled, with
> the plane on the runway- fueled up and ready to depart,
> but with its seats not completely filled. The incre-
> mental unit of service in this case might be defined
> as carrying of an extra passenger on that flight--in
> which case, the marginal cost would be practically
> zero. . . . Ideally, if the flight is going anyhow,

it is economically inefficient to turn away any pas-
senger willing to pay the marginal opportunity cost
of his trip—which is virtually zero <u>as long as there
are empty seats</u>. In short, the ideal remains pricing
at the shortest-run marginal cost for the smallest
possible increment of output [emphasis added].[24]

Returning to this theme a bit later:

In the case of the partly-empty airplane. . . the
"efficient price" would be zero as long as the response of travelers remained insufficient to fill
the plane; then it would have to jump the moment the
empty spaces fell one short of demand, possibly to
the full cost of an added flight but in any case to
whatever level necessary to equate the number of
available seats with the number of would-be passengers.
On each flight, the available seats would have to be
auctioned, with the uniform price settling at the
point required to clear the market.[25]

Would this uniform price (which could not be reached se-
quentially as passengers made their reservations) be equal to
marginal cost? We are looking at a right-angled marginal cost
function, which rises suddenly from zero to infinity (or any other
amount) as soon as short-run capacity is fully used. But when
vendors use price merely as a device for rationing a service, in
what sense is it equal to marginal cost? If demand is not sufficient to use up capacity, then price must be zero (assuming uniform price and recontracting by consumers). Marginal cost is also
zero. If demand exceeds capacity and sellers must ration the output, the price can be anything, depending on demand elasticity;
but marginal cost can also be anything, since it is a vertical function.
    This formulation tells us very little. Price in such circum-
stances is equal to marginal cost only by definition of marginal
cost as the short-run price that will ration the available supply.
Unfortunately if we define marginal cost as the incremental cost
of the "smallest possible" addition to supply, we are likely to
end up with these right-angle marginal cost functions lying along
zero in a vast number of cases. The very short run practically
requires them. And since real time is a sequence of these short-
run instants, we would practically take leave of "cost" in any
substantial sense as a guide to price.
    Notwithstanding this objection, short-run marginal cost even
as a simple reflection of limitation of supply will work out
pretty well in practice if <u>all</u> we expect from it is a short-run
rationing function. Under conditions of natural monopoly, a utility can adopt a strict market-efficiency approach to short-run
rationing even when uncertainties prevent it from confidently
melding a succession of short-run prices based on short-run marginal costs into a long-run income stream sufficient to cover

long-run costs. But for purposes of determining reasonable and
equitable price differentials in a discriminatory (value-of-ser-
vice) rate structure, with stable prices in the short run, it
is much less satisfactory. Here again equity and stability or
continuity appear as criteria of price performance, alongside
efficiency; continuous short-run marginal cost pricing will not
adequately satisfy those criteria. And for purposes of determining
permissible (nonpredatory) minimum prices in regulation of competition between a public utility and other enterprises, the
regulators are likely to find short-run marginal cost an erratic
instrument indeed.

Public utility regulation has had considerable experience with
minimum prices justified by short-run marginal costs, ranging
from the midnight tariffs in the days of railroad monopoly to the
promotional allowances by which electric utilities have tried
to buy business away from gas utilities and vice versa. Somehow,
in the view of the utilities, a competitive market always seems
to meet the test. One can usually find the right combination of
"givens," the necessary definition of the market, and a period
of the right length to produce a marginal cost less than the desired price, notwithstanding the rampant personal discrimination
that often results when these events are chained up in a time
sequence. The supporting economic theory assumes a timeless production process, without history, sequence, or future; homogeneity
in output; perfect mobility and frictionless access by customers
to a point market; perfect recontracting to reach perfect market
equilibrium; and so on. In a world in which these assumptions do
not correspond to fact, the principle of short-run marginal-cost
pricing can lead to bizarre results. In a disequilibrated world
of evolving events, inexact forecasts of an uncertain future,
and irretrievable decisions, short-run marginal cost appears, van-
ishes, changes its shape, shoots up to infinite space, crashes to
the ground, hides behind impenetrable disguises; no one really
knows what it is or where it is to be found. Business management
lives in a world in which none of these assumptions corresponds to
fact, and in the departures from these ideal conditions lie most
of the opportunities for price discrimination and most of the
controversies about minimum-cost tests.

Long-Run Marginal Costs in Data Communications

Even long-run marginal cost presents difficulties in definition
and application. For an example of the confusion possible in
application of the concept to the case of data transmission under
conditions of rivalry, we note a suggestion by AT&T that its incremental cost for data transmission services would be those of
the most efficient plant that it might employ in the future, even
though it might not install or use such plant during the next
decade. Thus, perhaps the cost of the waveguide facility ($1.02
per circuit mile) should be built into the criterion for minimum
price, in place of the T2 carrier ($7.39 per mile) which Bell and
its competitors will probably use.[26] Waveguide will not be ready

until 1978.

When economists speak of marginal costs, of course, they refer to actual use of resources, not an imaginary quantity embodying a vision of the future. AT&T hints that a low price will permit it (rather than its competitors) to realize rapid growth and the volume necessary to justify these facilities--in other words, that economies of scale are present after all. "Thus, diversion [to its competitors] of possible growth will result in either a delay in the introduction of a lower unit cost facility or the selection of a higher unit cost facility than would otherwise have been required."[27] This argument, and forecast, rationalizes a preemptive pricing strategy based on an intangible quantity, and if it should succeed, we may never know what the marginal cost actually is, nor whether economies of scale for waveguides are actually so great as to lead to natural monopoly in the end, nor whether one or more specialized competitors themselves would have succeeded in making a gradual transition to the later technology. The data transmission service would again have become firmly embedded within the monopoly frontier of the Bell System.

The "cream-skimming" argument seems particularly weak in this case, since the service does not actually exist and contributes nothing as yet to the Bell creamery. The natural monopoly phenomenon which must always be present in valid arguments against cream-skimming[28] is certainly not apparent to the unaided eye in digital transmission; if anything, the existing commitment of Bell to an analog network may inhibit its entry into a new, complete, competitive digital service. In this instance, the long-run effect of competitive entry would bring the benefits of new technology, with no discernible costs in the form of unnecessary duplication of service nor loss of the cost benefits of natural monopoly.

But other cases would not be so easy to decide. What is at issue is the location of the zone in which economies of scale and integration relative to the size of the market cease to be decisive. We have considered this question as it bears on voice and data communication services, but of course it also bears on other services and products that have been included within the corporate boundary of AT&T such as equipment produced by Western Electric, attachments and terminals that Bell insists upon supplying itself, research and development done in the Bell Laboratories, etc.[29] Within that zone the telephone network must be treated as an organic whole, free of selective competition from rivals who cannot realize equivalent economies of scale on limited portions of the business that look attractive because of the discriminatory rate structures that such regulated monopoly entities are encouraged--often required--to create.[30] Outside that zone, competition benefits the public. Yet unrestrained price rivalry is a poor way to determine where those areas actually are.

Perhaps we all can agree that it is neither logical nor workable to decide where regulation including limitations on entry should cease to apply by defining what is "communication" and what is not. Nor were all the issues in the data communications matter settled when the Federal Communications Commission decided not to

regulate data processing.[31] The precise roles of existing common
carriers, of new entrants to common carrier communications, and
of the data processors who wish to own and manage their own communications links still remain to be defined.

But this is only one of many possible examples of the difficulties that integration of diverse activities within a regulated
firm can lead to. They show up frequently within AT&T because of
its size and complexity; even so they would be much more numerous
if the Consent Decree of 1956 did not exclude AT&T from nonregulated markets outside the area of communications. Most large
utility enterprises exhibit similar problems, whenever the principles and tools used by regulators are not fully adaptable to
the total integrated enterprise that the regulators confront.
There are many corresponding problems in regulation of local electric and gas utilities, of natural gas pipelines, of transportation and communication. They tend to appear wherever a regulated
enterprise integrates activities not having public-utility characteristics with activities that do, or wherever it confronts a
free market in the midst of its regulated sectors, or wherever it
must divide an organically integrated activity between jurisdictions or between regulated and nonregulated sectors that throw an
arbitrary boundary line across the firm.

5. COMPETITION IN COMMUNICATIONS SATELLITES:
A STRUCTURAL DECISION

A further example of regulatory response to a complex structural
problem appeared as this essay was being completed: the decision
of the Federal Communications Commission on communications satellites. The FCC rejected the approach, urged on it by its staff,
that applicants for entry be required to combine into a single
"chosen instrument" franchised as a monopoly. Instead it decided
to allow all technically qualified applicants to enter and provide competitive services. All the same, the FCC felt it necessary to hedge the role of the leading competitors in various ways,
perhaps reflecting concerns similar to those that arise in other
parts of the communications system when competitors are admitted.

The FCC decision subjected AT&T and Communications Satellite
Corporation (Comsat) to the following restrictions:

(1) AT&T's initial satellite use will be limited to wide-area
telephone service (WATS), standby, and defense communications.

(2) Comsat may not provide service exclusively for AT&T,
though the latter can apply for its own satellite or lease one
from other carriers.

(3) If Comsat chooses to provide service for AT&T, it will
not be permitted to serve ultimate users, only communications
common carriers, and would be required to serve all such carriers
without discrimination and without devoting too much of its capacity to AT&T.

(4) Comsat will be required to form a separate corporate

subsidiary to provide domestic satellite services.

The commission expressed fears that AT&T's dominant position
would inhibit truly competitive entry into the satellite field;
also that its complex mixture of joint facilities and common costs
might conceal the true costs of satellite operations and lead to
subsidization of the competitive services with revenues from the
monopoly telephone services. These were much the same concerns
as those expressed above, for entry into digital communications.
The reaction of AT&T (and of Comsat) was also similar, decrying
"artificial restrictions" upon competition.[32]

The regulatory commission in this case does not think that
unrestrained competition in communications satellites will ensure
good economic performance. It is willing to take some chances
with economic efficiency in order to curb the market power of the
public utilities already established adjacent to the competitive
field. It may not believe that "efficiency" would result from
unrestrained market rivalry in any event.

Clearly, transfer of a previously regulated utility market to
the domain of competition would be no easier or simpler than
the demarcation of a new competitive service on the frontier of
established public utilities. The regulatory commissions, and the
policy-making legislative bodies behind them, face a highly complex situation which cannot be reduced to a simple binary choice
of "regulation" versus the "free market." And even if the authorities do decide to assign the activity to the form of strict control called public utility regulation, the regulatory process encounters similar complexities in the interior structure and en-
veloping markets of the regulated enterprise. As a rule, the regulatory authority finds no simple means of achieving optimum performance in terms of the accepted criteria for performance either
by regulating the decisions of the public utility firm or by ad-
mitting competitive pressures to its markets.

COMMENTS by Stanley G. Long

In his essay, Dean McKie states "The burden of proof of natural
monopoly in any activity that the utility wishes to undertake
exclusively must be sustained by demonstrable facts." I agree,
but except for a fleeting caveat he does not demonstrate to me
during his discussion that he really believes this. Put in slightly different terms, Dean McKie is much more willing to accept the
institutional status quo in public utility regulation as given
than am I--he does not follow through with the skepticism about
present regulatory practice that the "burden of proof" quote
would seem to call for, and he seems to accept implicitly the

existence of regulation as evidence that such regulation is "necessary" and that natural monopoly exists in that part of the
economy.

I should like to mention several themes in the literature on
monopoly and regulation which suggest to me strong doubts about
the effectiveness of regulation as the appropriate instrument
of social control in many cases where it is now used or advocated.

First, there is the "captive regulatory agency" hypothesis:
the proposition is, roughly, that with or without the presence of
well-intentioned men as commissioners, regulatory agencies tend
to identify with the interests of the firms they are supposed
to be protecting us from rather than with consumer welfare. This
hypothesis is discussed in four articles, three of which appeared
in the New Individualist Review 2, no. 4 (1962). They are:
Christopher D. Stone's "ICC: Some Reminiscence on the Future
of American Transportation," Sam Peltzman's "CAB: Freedom from
Competition," and Robert M. Hunt's "FCC: Free Speech, Public
Needs and Mr. Minow." The fourth article is George J. Stigler's
"Theory of Regulation" (Bell Journal of Economics and Management
Science, Spring 1971, pp. 3-21).

A second theme in the literature on monopoly and regulation
is the analysis that welfare loss from unregulated monopoly power
may be small. This is discussed in Richard A. Posner's "Natural
Monopoly and Its Regulation" (Stanford Law Review, February 1969).
Especially, in the long run, as pointed out in Joseph Schumpeter's
Capitalism, Socialism and Democracy (New York: Harper and Brothers,
1950), any given firm's monopoly power may be transitory, whereas
regulation may perpetuate noncompetitive performance. There is also the proposition set forth in Harold Demsetz's "Why Regulate
Utilities?" (Journal of Law and Economics, April 1968, pp. 55-65)
that even if the cost conditions of production call for only one
firm rather than many, this does not preclude competition in the
competitive pricing of the output among several potential producers.
Finally, in George J. Stigler's and Claire Friedland's "What
Can Regulators Regulate? The Case of Electricity" (Journal of
Law and Economics, October 1962, pp. 1-16) the question has been
raised whether or not regulation has any of the effects on prices
and profits commonly attributed to it.

I should admit candidly that my reconsideration of the regulatory process in preparation for this conference has made me
doubtful about its effectiveness. At the very minimum it seems
to me that institutional inertia (the tyranny of the status quo
and the near irreversibility of new agency regulatory activities,
once begun) should make us hesitate before opting for regulation
in new situations such as those cited by Dean McKie in his essay--
data communications, communications satellites, etc. Dean McKie
in his "Regulatory Boundaries" (Bell Journal of Economics and
Management Science, Spring 1970, pp. 6-26) has written of the "tar-
baby effect"--the tendency of regulatory activity to spread.

I suggest that if several firms wish to "get into the act"
that this may be prima facie evidence that natural monopoly
does not exist. And, if the would-be entrants optimistically

guessed wrong and some should lose claim to their resources this may be a small and visible cost to pay to avoid the indefinite institutionalization of relatively hard-to-see inefficiency under the regulatory umbrella.

I would like you to try to imagine with me what telephone technology and industrial structure might be like today if there had never been regulation. Possibly it might still cost $20.00 to telephone coast to coast. If it did, I would wager that many efficient message alternatives, in addition to a vigorous Western Union system, would be available. On the other hand, perhaps my telephone set today would have no wires and would be wristwatch sized. Or, we may conjecture, I might be able to purchase service into a communications network that would be unavailable to encyclopedia salesmen. Without excessive flights of imagination, we may suppose that the technology of the industry would likely be very different than it is and it is not at all clear that such a different technology would be incompatible with the coexistence of several competing firms, especially if all scarce resources, including the rights to uglification of the cityscape with wires and poles, and the rights to use particular radio "channels" or wavelengths had been auctioned off competitively rather than given away by a political agency, when a franchise containing elements of monopoly power was bestowed.

I have no quarrel with Dean McKie's "policy standards" of static efficiency, progress, equity. Like apple pie these values are probably widely accepted--for all industries, not just for utilities or pseudo-utilities. I simply question if regulation is always the appropriate means to these ends, even for those firms, if any, that are without question natural monopolies. A fortiori, where there is some question as to whether natural monopoly is present there are serious doubts.

Regarding the "policy standards" of stability and continuity of service it seems to me that governmental standards about product quality are set throughout the economy and that these issues are not really part of the question of regulation per se. Thus, the U.S.D.A. places standards on meat, there are housing codes, automobile safety codes, minimum professional standards, etc., and quality standards are often set regardless of the structure of the producing industry.

It is true, if easy to say, that the "boundary problem" would disappear if regulation ceased. What we would still have to cope with would be the problem of analyzing a multiproduct or conglomerate firm. If predatory noncompetition or other evils of economic giantism were then shown to exist, they would fall under the domain of antitrust policy and/or tax reform.

As a concluding remark, if regulation deliberately redistributes income, or subsidizes services that would not pay their way but which would be justified on such grounds as external benefits, I would greatly prefer to see such subsidies made directly and explicitly rather than as by-products of regulation.

NOTES / INDEX

Notes

1. Public Utilities and the Theory of Power

1. See, among others, Lee Loevinger, "Regulation and Compe-
tition as Alternatives," Antitrust Bulletin 11, nos. 1 and 2
(January-April 1966): 101; Charles Donahue, Jr., "Lawyers,
Economists, and the Regulated Industries: Thoughts on Profes-
sional Roles Inspired by Some Recent Economic Literature,"
Michigan Law Review 70 (1971): 195; Joseph J. Spengler, "Evolution of Public-Utility Industry Regulation: Economists and Other
Determinants," South African Journal of Economics 37, no. 1 (March
1969): 3; and Joseph J. Spengler, "The Public Utility Problem
Viewed Historically," in A Critique of Administrative Regulation
of Public Utilities, ed. Harry M. Trebing and Warren J. Samuels
(East Lansing: Institute of Public Utilities, 1972), and the
comments thereon by Ben Lewis and Warren J. Samuels.
2. The qualifications of the conventional economic paradigm
are partly surveyed and interpreted in Warren J. Samuels, "Welfare Economics, Power and Property," in Perspectives of Property,
ed. Gene Wunderlich and W. L. Gibson, Jr. (University Park: Institute for Research on Land and Water Resources, Pennsylvania
State University Press, 1972), and in the Comments by Lewis and
Samuels on Spengler, "The Public Utility Problem Viewed
Historically."
3. This paradigm represents a partial integration and extension of earlier work of mine. On the general theory of choice
and power, see "The Nature and Scope of Economic Policy," Appendix
in Warren J. Samuels, The Classical Theory of Economic Policy
(Cleveland: World Press, 1966). On the specific paradigm of power
and mutual coercion, see Samuels, "Welfare Economics, Power and
Property." On the analysis of subprocesses in terms of power (and
an interpretation of the theory of power as a second tradition
within economics), see Warren J. Samuels, "The Scope of Economics
Historically Considered," Land Economics 48 (August 1972): 248-
68. On the interrelation between legal and market processes, see
Warren J. Samuels, "Interrelations between Legal and Economic
Processes," Journal of Law and Economics 14, no. 2 (October 1971):

435, and, with a reinterpretation of the history of economic
thought in respect to the role of government, Warren J. Samuels,
"Government in the History of Economics," mimeographed (East
Lansing: Michigan State University, 1972). The analysis is
deeply influenced by the work in legal economics and public util-
ities of Robert Lee Hale. See Warren J. Samuels, "The Economy as
a System of Power and Its Legal Bases: The Legal Economics of
Robert Lee Hale," mimeographed (East Lansing: Michigan State
University, 1972); and John Maurice Clark, Social Control of
Business, 2d ed. (New York: McGraw-Hill, 1939), which adopts
much of Hale's basic paradigm and thrust; as well as the work of
John R. Commons, Edwin E. Witte, and Frank H. Knight.

4. This and the discussion following in the text represent
an extension and elaboration of the argument in Warren J. Samuels,
"Theory of Regulation in Relation to Return," Public Utilities
Fortnightly, November 9, 1967, p. 47.

5. Public utility regulation has become "imbedded in certain
categories which in turn" have "limited the questions asked of
regulation and the answers admitted," pretending to give complete
and self-sufficient answers but actually only answers on its own
terms to the questions which those terms allowed. Spengler, "The
Public Utility Problem Viewed Historically"; and G. L. S. Shackle,
The Years of High Theory (New York: Cambridge University Press,
1967), p. 5.

6. Samuels, "Theory of Regulation in Relation to Return,"
November 9, 1967.

7. Ibid., p. 53.

8. See, among others, John H. Gray and Jack Levin, The Valuation and Regulation of Public Utilities (New York: Harper, 1933),
Chs. 1, 8-10.

9. See Loevinger, "Regulation and Competition as Alternatives,"
p. 129.

10. See the quotation from Machlup, in Samuels, "Theory of
Regulation in Relation to Return," November 23, 1967, pp. 36, 38.

11. On the desideratum of reasonable acceptance of regulation
by the industry, see William L. Cary, Politics and the Regulatory
Agencies (New York: McGraw-Hill, 1967), pp. 2, 61, 63, 69, 73,
81, 95, 98, 110. For the view that government is not independent
and exogenous, and that business is not tyrannized but brought
within regulation as part of the self-governing population, see
Warren J. Samuels, "Edwin E. Witte's Concept of the Role of Government in the Economy," Land Economics 43 (May 1967): 131, 134-
35, 139, 140, 141, 144.

12. Samuels, "Theory of Regulation in Relation to Return,"
November 23, 1967, p. 38; Marver H. Bernstein, "Independent Regu-
latory Agencies: A Perspective on Their Reform," in Trebing and
Samuels, A Critique of Administrative Regulation of Public Util-
ities; and Merle Fainsod, "Some Reflections on the Nature of the
Regulatory Press," in Public Policy, ed. C. J. Friedrich and E. S.
Mason (Cambridge: Harvard University Press, 1940), pp. 279-323.

13. See Bernstein, "Independent Regulatory Agencies"; Cary,
Politics and the Regulatory Agencies; Loevinger, "Regulation and

Competition as Alternatives"; and the Comments by Lewis on Spengler,
"Evolution of Public-Utility Industry Regulation" and on Spengler,
"The Public Utility Problem Viewed Historically," See also Horace
M. Gray, "The Passing of the Public Utility Concept," Land Econo-
mics 16 (February 1940), reprinted in Readings in the Social Con-
trol of Industry (Philadelphia: Blakiston, for the American
Economic Association, 1949), pp. 280-303; and Spengler's articles
"Evolution of Public-Utility Industry Regulation" and "The Public
Utility Problem Viewed Historically."

14. See, e.g., Loevinger, "Regulation and Competition as Alternatives," p. 118.

15. See George J. Stigler and Claire Friedland, "What can
Regulators Regulate? The Case of Electricity," Journal of Law and
Economics 5 (October 1962): 1.

16. See Cary, Politics and the Regulatory Agencies; and
Manuel F. Cohen and George J. Stigler, Can Regulatory Agencies
Protect Consumers? (Washington, D.C.: American Enterprise Insti-
tute for Public Policy Research, 1971), p. 58, et passim.

17. Both the demand for regulation and the demand for deregulation are demands for particular rights; the demand for rights is
a demand for government, with the differences between the rights
demanded amounting to differences in the uses to which government
would be put.

18. Regulation and the law of property (or property rights)
are functionally equivalent in that (a) both structure power in
and through the market, (b) both primarily represent established
rights, (c) both involve the problem of continuity versus change
of rights, (d) both involve the problem of the selective identification of rights both as rights and as good or bad, (e) both
require, with respect to efficiency solutions, antecedent deter-
minations of who is to count, and (f) both are objects of manipulation as power players attempt to use government as an economic
alternative for their own ends.

19. Richard A. Posner, "Taxation by Regulation," Bell Journal
of Economics and Management Science 2, no. 1 (Spring 1971): 22;
and Donahue, Jr., "Lawyers, Economists, and the Regulated Industries," p. 10.

20. Joseph A. Schumpeter, "The Crisis of the Tax State,"
International Economic Papers 4 (1954): 17.

21. Roger Noll, "The Economics and Politics of Regulation,"
Virginia Law Review 47, no. 6 (September 1971): 1016, 1029.

22. "The Administrative Process is a governmental tool. It
is no more conservative or liberal than the elevator in the Senate
Office Building. It is used to promote pro-business policies,
anti-business policies, and policies having little or nothing to
do with business. It has often been used as an instrument of law
reform, but it is also used as a means of protecting vested interests. . . . Although the administrative process is politically
colorless in that it has no distinctive political character of its
own, it does have a peculiar chameleonic quality of taking on the
color of the substantive program to which it is attached, and it
is always attached to a substantive program." Kenneth Culp Davis,

p. 6, excerpted in The Politics of Regulation, ed. Samuel Krislov
and Lloyd D. Musolf (Boston: Houghton Mifflin, 1964), p. 220.

23. See W. H. Hutt, Economists and the Public (London:
Jonathan Cape, 1936), Chs. 3, 4, et passim.

24. Harold Demsetz, "Why Regulate Utilities?" Journal of Law
and Economics 11 (April 1968): 55, 65. "Regulation may be actively sought by an industry, or it may be thrust upon it. A central thesis of this paper is that, as a rule, regulation is
acquired by the industry and is designed and operated primarily
for its benefit." George J. Stigler, "The Theory of Economic
Regulation," Bell Journal of Economics and Management Science 2,
no. 1 (Spring 1971): 3, cf. 4, 5, 10. The classic statements are
by Gray, "The Passing of the Public Utility Concept," and Marver
H. Bernstein, Regulating Business By Independent Commission
(Princeton: Princeton University Press, 1955). See also James
Q. Wilson, "The Dead Hand of Regulation," Public Interest, no.
25 (Fall 1971), p. 39; Richard A. Posner, "Power in America,"
Public Interest, no. 25 (Fall 1971), p. 114; and Richard A.
Posner, "Natural Monopoly and Its Regulation," Stanford Law
Review 21, no. 3 (February 1969): 548.

25. See Stigler, "The Theory of Economic Regulation," pp. 11,
17, 18; and Noll, "The Economics and Politics of Regulation,"
pp. 1030, 1031. The general principle that government is an instrument of the powerful (in a general interdependence system),
including those most readily organized, is not vitiated (only
shown to be a tendency) by the fact that government is also used
to protect the powerless and the poor. One of the major chapters
in the history of the modern state is the operation of conscience
and moral suasion upon and through the state; public opinion, as
de Tocqueville perceived, is very important here. Nonetheless,
reform movements and subsidy programs ostensibly directed to help
the weak and the poor typically benefit the non-weak and the non-
poor more.

26. Cohen and Stigler, Can Regulatory Agencies Protect Con-
sumers? pp. 48, 56, 67, 80; and Louis L. Jaffe, "The Effective
Limits of the Administrative Process: A Reevaluation," Harvard
Law Review 67 (May 1954): 1105, 1113.

27. Mark J. Green et al., The Closed Enterprise System (New
York: Grossman, 1972), p. ix; also see the review in Newsweek,
June 14, 1971, p. 86.

28. Posner, "Taxation by Regulation"; and Alfred Rappaport,
"Regulation, Rate Making and Modes of Rationality," paper used
at Conference on Current Issues in Public Utility Management and
Regulation, August 30, 1971, at Northwestern University, p. 13.

29. Warren J. Samuels, "Public Utility Holding Companies and
Housing," Public Utilities Fortnightly, May 25, 1972, pp. 16-22.

30. Noll, "The Economics and Politics of Regulation," pp.
1025, 1026, 1028 ff.

31. Ibid., pp. 1018 ff.

32. Loevinger, "Regulation and Competition as Alternatives,"
pp. 122, 123, 131-32.

33. Noll, "The Economics and Politics of Regulation," p. 1022.

34. Robert Fellmeth, The Interstate Commerce Omission (New York: Grossman, 1970), p. vii.

35. George W. Hilton, "The Basic Behavior of Regulatory Commissions," American Economic Review, Papers and Proceedings 62 (May 1972): 47, 50, 52; Posner, "Natural Monopoly and Regulation"; and Noll, "The Economics and Politics of Regulation," p. 1027.

36. Edward F. Cox et al., Report on the Federal Trade Commission (New York: Grove Press, 1969), pp. 63, 68, et passim; Nicholas Johnson, "A New Fidelity to the Regulatory Ideal," Georgetown Law Journal 59, no. 4 (March 1971): 869, 900 n. 32; and Samuels, "Theory of Regulation in Relation to Return," November 9, 1967, p. 58 n. 10, et passim.

37. Samuels, "Theory of Regulation in Relation to Return," November 9, 1967, p. 56 and n. 49.

38. Ibid., November 23, 1967, pp. 36-37; Samuels, "On the Effect of Regulation on Value"; and Noll, "The Economics and Politics of Regulation," p. 1027.

39. See, e.g., William A. Jordan, Airline Regulation in America (Baltimore: Johns Hopkins Press, 1970).

40. Bernstein, Regulating Business By Independent Commission, p. 265.

41. Wilson, "The Dead Hand of Regulation," pp. 47, 57; Loevinger, "Regulation and Competition as Alternatives," pp. 122, 130.

42. Loevinger, "Regulation and Competition as Alternatives," p. 122.

43. Cohen and Stigler, Can Regulatory Agencies Protect Consumers? pp. 6 ff., 17, 74, 80.

44. "What the world of American Capitalism actually sought was a set of precepts according to which government as a restrictive entity would be kept on the defensive, while at the same time government as an ally would not be discouraged. It follows that the real contribution of the public utility concept to economic, political, and social development in this country lay precisely in the manner in which it operated to keep restrictive control on the defensive while at the same time allowing overt recognition of the necessity for some such control." Howard R. Smith, "The Rise and Fall of the Public Utility Concept," Journal of Land and Public Utility Economics 23 (1947): 117, 120. See also Johnson, "A New Fidelity to the Regulatory Ideal," p. 874.

45. Rappaport, "Regulation, Rate Making and Modes of Rationality."

46. Jaffe, "The Effective Limits of the Administrative Process," pp. 1113, 1115, 1117, 1135; Noll, "The Economics and Politics of Regulation"; Stigler, "The Theory of Economic Regulation"; Gray and Levin, The Valuation and Regulation of Public Utilities, p. 124, et passim; and Krislov and Musolf, The Politics of Regulation, p. 50.

47. "The agencies themselves will become preoccupied with the details of regulation and the minutiae of cases in whatever form they first inherit them, trying by the slow manipulation of details to achieve various particular effects that happen to

commend themselves from time to time to various agency members."
Wilson, "The Dead Hand of Regulation," pp. 47-48. "An agency that
makes decisions to minimize the chance of being overruled by subsequent legal or legislative decisions will tend to be overly
responsive to the interests of the regulated. First, giving the
regulated industry something more than it deserves means that the
industry has something to lose if it appeals. Second, the agency
will want to be sure that it cannot legitimately be accused of
being unfair to the groups most likely to challenge the decision.
Third, most of the information flowing to the agency will come
from the regulated, who normally can afford to employ better
resources than can the representatives of the general public."
Noll, "The Economics and Politics of Regulation," p. 1030. See
also Hilton, "The Basic Behavior of Regulatory Commissions," pp.
48 ff.

    48. Cary, Politics and the Regulatory Agencies, pp. 10-11,
67, 136.

    49. Jaffe, "The Effective Limits of the Administrative Pro-
cess," p. 1114.

    50. See, for example, the address of George I. Bloom, Presi-
dent, National Association of Regulatory Utility Commissioners
(NARUC) before the Midwest Association of Railroad and Utilities
Commissioners, Topika, Kansas, June 14, 1971, p. 7 of mimeographed
text: "The agencies are not so much industry-oriented or
consumer-oriented as regulation-oriented. They are in the regulation business, and regulate they will, with or without a rationale"
(Wilson, "The Dead Hand of Regulation," p. 48).

    51. Bloom, address before the Midwest Association of Railroad
and Utilities Commissioners, p. 5.

    52. Jaffe, "The Effective Limits of the Administrative Pro-
cess," p. 1113.

    53. Samuels, "Theory of Regulation in Relation to Return."

    54. Noll, "The Economics and Politics of Regulation," p. 1029.

    55. Spengler, "Evolution of Public-Utility Industry Regula-
tion," p. 15.

    56. Gray, "The Passing of the Public Utility Concept," pp.
294-95.

    57. Johnson, "A New Fidelity to the Regulatory Ideal," pp.
876 ff.

    58. Jaffe, "The Effective Limits of the Administrative Pro-
cess," p. 1131.

    59. Cary, Politics and the Regulatory Agencies, pp. 18, 42,
51, 66, 69.

    60. Joseph C. Goulden, The Superlawyers (New York: Weibright
and Talley, 1972), reviewed in Newsweek, May 14, 1972.

    61. Gray and Levin, The Valuation and Regulation of Public
Utilities, pp. 116, 119, et passim; and Johnson, "A New Fidelity
to the Regulatory Ideal," p. 889. Environmentalist groups have
become rather effective in using the technique widely pursued by
utilities throughout the history of regulation.

    62. Jaffe, "The Effective Limits of the Administrative Pro-
cess," pp. 1133, 1135.

63. John M. Kyhlman and Terry D. David, "The Automobile-Rental Industry: An Economic Analysis of the Airport 'Concessionaire' Agreement," Antitrust Law and Economics Review 5 (1971): 59.

64. Samuels, "Theory of Regulation in Relation to Return," November 9, 1967, p. 54.

65. Carl A. Auerbach, "Pluralism and the Administrative Process," Annals of the American Academy of Political and Social Science 400 (March 1972): 1, 12, 13.

66. Ibid., p. 12.

67. James L. Sundquist, quoted in Annals of the American Academy of Political and Social Science 400, p. 8.

68. Samuels, "Theory of Regulation in Relation to Return," November 9, 1967, pp. 52, 55.

69. Cary, Politics and the Regulatory Agencies, e.g., pp. 93, 106.

70. Auerbach, "Pluralism and the Administrative Process," p. 13.

71. Cox et al., Report on the Federal Trade Commission, p. xii.

72. Samuels, "Theory of Regulation in Relation to Return," November 9, 1967, pp. 55-56.

73. Loevinger, "Regulation and Competition as Alternatives," p. 124.

74. Robert A. Solo, Economic Organizations and Social Systems (Indianapolis: Bobbs-Meriill, 1967), p. 215.

75. Samuels, "On the Effect of Regulation on Value," p. 21.

76. Warren J. Samuels, The Classical Theory of Economic Policy (Cleveland: World Press, 1966), pp. 277-78.

77. Loevinger, "Regulation and Competition as Alternatives," p. 131.

78. Rappaport, "Regulation, Rate Making and Modes of Rationality," p. 35, et passim.

2. Practical Economics of Public Utility Regulation

1. The policies and opinions reflected herein are solely those of the author and do not reflect in any way the policy positions of the Federal Power Commission.

2. H. Averch and L. L. Johnson, "Behavior of the Firm under Regulatory Constraint," American Economic Review 52, no. 5 (December 1962): 1053-69.

3. W. Baumol and A. Klevorick, "The Averch-Johnson Thesis," Bell Journal of Economics and Management Science 1, no. 2 (Autumn 1970): 162-90.

4. Stanislaw H. Wellisz, "Regulation of Natural Gas Pipeline Companies: An Economic Analysis," Journal of Political Economy 71, no. 1 (February 1963): 30-43.

5. Alfred E. Kahn, The Economics of Regulation: Principles and Institutions (New York: John Wiley & Sons, 1971), 2: 106.

6. Averch and Johnson, "Behavior of the Firm under Regulatory

Constraint," p. 1053.

7. E. E. Zajac, "A Geometric Treatment of Averch–Johnson's Behavior of the Firm Model," American Economic Review 60, No. 1 (March 1970): 117–25.

8. Of course, the profit function of the regulated utility is assumed to have all of the desirable convexities and properties for profit maximization calculations in accordance with the traditional theory of the firm.

9. Zajac, "A Geometric Treatment of Averch–Johnson's Behavior of the Firm Model," pp. 119–20.

10. Cf. E. Bailey and R. Coleman, "The Effect of Lagged Regulation in an Averch–Johnson Model," Bell Journal of Economics and Management Science 2, no. 1 (Spring 1971): 278–92; and Kahn, The Economics of Regulation, p. 106

11. For example, Bailey and Coleman, "The Effect of Lagged Regulation in an Averch–Johnson Model," assumed that the lag period was of constant duration.

12. Wellisz, "Regulation of Natural Gas Pipeline Companies," pp. 30–43 cf. P. O. Steiner, "Peak Loads and Efficient Pricing," Quarterly Journal of Economics 71, no. 4 (November 1957): 585–610; O. E. Williamson, "Peak Load Pricing and Optimal Capacity," American Economic Review 56, no. 4, pt. 1 (September 1966): 810–27; James M. Buchanan, "Peak Loads and Efficient Pricing: Comment," Quarterly Journal of Economics 72, no. 3 (August 1958): 451–62; P. O. Steiner, "Peak Load Pricing Revisited," in Essays on Public Utility Pricing and Regulation, ed. Harry M. Trebing (East Lansing: Michigan State University, 1971), pp. 3–21.

13. Of course D'D' can intersect the OQ axis at some point greater than B and the marginal cost price of off-peak demand would then be greater than zero.

14. Wellisz, "Regulation of Natural Gas Pipeline Companies," p. 35.

15. The welfare loss of the OB' output under rate of return regulation is GHD' (which is the excess of the off-peak customers' loss over the revenues collected from them) + NLS (which is the excess of the cost of peak service over the premium paid for that service) assuming no income distribution effect.

16. The FPC has tilted the rate structure away from the Seaboard Formula by allocating smaller percentages than 50 percent of the fixed costs to the commodity charge on the basis of interfuel competition. Cf. Natural Gas Pipeline Company of America, FPC Docket No. RP61-8, Opinion and Order, October 25, 1972. In reference to the impact of higher gas prices on Peoples Gas Light and Coke Co.'s ability to compete with coal for industrial sales if Natural's commodity charge were increased, the opinion stated that the "loss of such sales would decidedly not be in the public interest."

17. There is no evidence that pipelines choose capacity over storage because it represents a large rate base technology, but that could be an influence.

18. Since the incentives for buying cheaper off-peak gas and storing it are stronger for the distributor, this development is

not surprising and is still in the best interest of developing a well-balanced system.

19. Some of these industrial sales are firm sales as well as interruptible.

20. At least two pipelines, but probably more, are curtailing gas during the off-peak season presently in order to inject gas into storage.

21. Cf. Fred A. Thornton, "FPC Allocation of Gas Storage Costs," Public Utilities Fortnightly, May 25, 1972, pp. 11-15.

22. Although there is presently no basis for a definite conclusion concerning technology choices, there is at least presently no evidence that pipelines choose large capital investment in pipeline capacity over smaller, more efficient investments in storage because of the A-J influences.

3. Investment Characteristics of Common Stocks

1. The author wishes to acknowledge the programming assistance of Marvin Lipson and Jules Kamin. The data analyzed in this essay were either compiled for the Center for Research in Security Prices (CRSP), Graduate School of Business, University of Chicago, or were compiled under the Center's auspices.

2. Preliminary examination of the extended data file suggests that results for the most recent period, although useful for the purposes of this essay, will be subject to somewhat more revision than results through June 1968. One recently discovered error, for example, is that the December 1971 prices are for the 30th rather than the 31st.

3. Appendix tables containing indexes, relatives, and counts for market, nonregulated, regulated, transportation, utilities, and communications groupings, and a complete listing of the regulated companies entering the analysis are available from the author. These tables were omitted here to conserve space.

4. This is the author's first venture into the field of public utility economics. He cannot hope to conceal his ignorance of its literature. If the ideas presented in this section are either novel or interesting, they might be developed further.

5. Merton H. Miller and Franco Modigliani, "Dividend Policy, Growth, and the Valuation of Shares," Journal of Business 34, no. 4 (October 1971): 411-33.

6. See Lawrence Fisher, "Some New Stock Market Indexes," Journal of Business 39, no. 1 (January 1966): 191-225.

7. Each edition of the CRSP Investment Return File was compiled from the then most recent edition of the CRSP Master File, which I had compiled through 1965. More recent data were collected by Portland State University and by Willamette Management Associates. The original CRSP computer programs were used now updating through the 1970 edition. A new set of programs, intended for nearly continuous updating and coded by the staff of Interactive

Data Corporation, was used for the most recent update.

These files were originally developed at the University of Chicago. Since 1967 they have been owned by subsidiaries of Standard & Poor's Corporation. They are available at a very substantial price from Standard & Poor's Automated Pricing Services, 345 Hudson Street, New York, New York 10014.

8. The original form of the Master File is described in Lawrence Fisher and James H. Lorie, "Rates of Return on Investments in Common Stocks," Journal of Business 37, no. 1 (January 1964): 1–21. The current form is described in the pamphlet CRSP Master File, prepared by Standard & Poor's Corporation, 1972.

9. There are some good reasons for this disappearance. One of the major reasons that the Return File was developed was for computing investment performance indexes of the type suggested by Kalman J. Cohen and Bruce P. Fitch, "The Average Investment Performance Index," Management Science 12 (February 1966): 195–215; and which was reported in Lawrence Fisher, "Some New Stock Market Indexes," Journal of Business 39, no. 1 (January 1966): 191–225. In these indexes each security's percentage-return performance receives equal weight--i.e., a weight that does not depend on either the size of the firm or the number of shares into which the firm's equity happens to be divided. Since an agreement to merge usually precedes the actual exchange of stock, to have counted both of the stocks that were merged together for the month in which the merger was consummated would have resulted in double counting which is undesirable. It would have been possible to include the successor's performance as part of the record of the stock that had disappeared; but, if I had done so I would have included data that were not to be used in making the monthly indexes. The other major initial purpose of the Return File was for the computations reported in Lawrence Fisher, "Outcomes for 'Random' Investments in Common Stocks Listed on the New York Stock Exchange," Journal of Business 38, no. 2 (April 1965): 149–61. These computations showed the probability distribution of outcomes from selecting a stock, a purchase month, and a subsequent sale month at random. To have included data for a stock after it had been merged into another would have resulted in excessive lack of independence in the sampling process. Therefore at the time the Return File was first produced (1964) it did not seem worthwhile to incur the very substantial expense needed to make the Return File follow stocks past the point of delisting. However, this property of the Return File is a bad one for the study reported here.

10. See the following articles by Lawrence Fisher and James H. Lorie: "Rates of Return on Investments in Common Stocks," Journal of Business 37, no. 1 (January 1964): 1–21; "Rates of Return on Investments in Common Stock: The Year-by-Year Record, 1926–65," Journal of Business 39, no. 1 (January 1966): 291–316; and "Some Studies of Variability of Returns on Investments in Common Stocks," Journal of Business 43, no. 2 (April 1970): 99–134.

11. Another source of difference is that brokerage commissions

are taken into account in the rates of return and wealth ratios reported in the articles by Fisher and Lorie cited in note 10 above. The calculations based on indexes omit their consideration--partly because monthly revision of the composition of the portfolio in the manner implied by chaining the link relatives of the index would be a very costly, and probably very foolish, policy if one had to take commissions into account. The differences introduced by neglecting commissions amount to about 1 percent of the wealth ratio for the "cash-to-portfolio" cases of the above articles.

12.   Cited in note 6 above.

13.   Cited in note 10 above.

14.   Still another possible source of difference is genuine bias that is caused by errors in the data used in compilation of the index. However, in Fisher, "Some New Stock Market Indexes," I thought the errors were small in their cumulative effect; and this still appears to be the case. For example, in the original calculation of the Arithmetic Investment Performance Index, the value for January 1926 was 1.59 (December 1960 = 100). It was found after thousands of revisions in the data and after rewriting the computer program that makes the Return File in order to use a more sophisticated algorithm. This change alters the implicit rate of return for the 34 and 11/12 years from January 1926 to December 1960 by less than 0.1 percent per annum. Moreover, the most of this change appears to be due to the change in the method of computation and not to changes in the underlying data.

15.   Fisher and Lorie, "Some Studies of Variability of Returns on Investments in Common Stocks."

16.   See, for example, Paol L. Cheng and M. King Deets, "Statistical Biases and Security Rates of Return," Journal of Financial and Quantitative Analysis 6, no. 3 (June 1971): 977-94.

17.   Marshall Blume, "Unbiased Estimators of Long Run Expected Rate of Return." Working Paper No. 19-72 presented to the Symposium on Modern Capital Theory (August 1972), sponsored by the Wells Fargo Bank.

18.   See Harry Markowitz, Portfolio Selection, Efficient Diversification of Investments (New York: John Wiley & Sons, 1959), and William F. Sharpe, "A Simplified Model for Portfolio Analysis," Management Science 9 (January 1963): 277-93.

19.   See William F. Sharpe, "Capital Asset Prices: A Theory of Market Equllibrium Under Conditions of Risk," Journal of Finance 19, no. 3 (September 1964): 425-42.

20.   See Lawrence Fisher, "The Estimation of Systematic Risk: Some New Findings," Proceedings on the Seminar on the Analysis of Security Prices (Chicago: University of Chicago, Center for Research in Security Prices, May 1970); idem, "On the Estimation of Systematic Risk," paper presented to the Symposium on Modern Capital Theory, July 1971, sponsored by Wells Fargo Bank and held in San Francisco; and Lawrence Fisher and Jules Kamin, "Good Betas and Bad Betas: How to Tell the Difference," Proceedings of the Seminar on the Analysis of Security Prices (Chicago: University of Chicago, Center for Research in Security Prices, November 1971).

21. Recall that in table 2, rates for the 11 months (January 30-December 31, 1926) have been converted to annual rates.

22. Because of errors that have now been corrected, the revised rate for 1936 differs substantially from Fisher and Lorie, "Rates of Return on Investments in Common Stock: The Year-by-Year Record, 1926-65."

23. See Richard Roll, "Bias in Fitting the Sharpe Model to Time Series Data," Journal of Financial and Quantitative Analysis 4, no. 3 (September 1969).

4. Public Utility Regulation

1. The research on which this article is based was carried on as part of the Program of Studies in the Regulation of Economic Activity of the Brookings Institution, Washington, D.C.

2. Cf. William Iulo, "Problems in the Definition and Measurements of Superior Performance," in Performance Under Regulation, ed. Harry M. Trebing (East Lansing: Michigan State University, 1968), pp. 3-19; and William H. Dodge, "Productivity Measures and Performance Evaluation," ibid., pp. 20-32.

3. Cf. William Capron, ed., Technological Change in Regulated Industries (Washington, D.C.: Brookings Institution, 1971).

4. See the contributions of Boiteux and other Tarif Vert theorists in Marginal Cost Pricing in Practice, ed. James R. Nelson (Englewood Cliffs, N.J.: Prentice-Hall, 1964); also Fred M. Westfield, "Practicing Marginal-Cost Pricing--A Review," Journal of Business 39, no. 1 (January 1966). (Tarif Vert is the French electric power tariff, so called from its green cover, based on an approach to pricing worked out by Boiteux, et al.)

5. These are all properties of the "boundary problem." Cf. James W. McKie, "Regulation and the Free Market: The Problem of Boundaries," Bell Journal of Economics and Management Science 1, no. 1 (Spring 1970): 6-26.

6. For a more extended discussion including several examples, see Bell Journal of Economics and Management Science 1, no. 1, pp. 17-19. Railroad competition between terminals in the days of railroad monopoly is a classic case.

7. The theoretical Tarif Vert approach (prices always equal to short-run marginal cost or SRMC) would produce adequate revenue when demand is correctly forecast as a guide to installation of the correct amount of capacity in the long run. But it would really require the freedom and protection of natural monopoly to work effectively; one of the problems with price rivalry between utilities is that neither demand forecasts nor calculation of elasticities in the disputed area are possible. Another is the constant temptation to price below SRMC for strategic reasons, or else to use a special definition of SRMC for each competitive situation.

8. Recently, for example, the ICC felt it necessary to limit

the use of proceeds from a $6 million issue of short-term notes
by the Western Pacific Railroad to railroad purposes only. "The
conditions reflect the Commission's growing concern over a drain
of assets from railroad to other functions. The drain has been
especially accelerated in recent years by railroad formation of
holding companies to foster diversification into more profitable
lines of business." Wall Street Journal, February 11, 1970, p. 21.

9. For example, a message from a branch office notifying a
central sales office that a sale has taken place can also be
switched to inventory control, which enters it and subtracts the
quantity from the total in the computer memory (processing) and
can then send back the subtraction to the order department as
a message to replenish inventory (reverse communication and
further switching), all directed by a machine program.

10. "[We] are prepared to render ad hoc evaluations with
respect to 'hybrid services' to determine whether a particular
package service is essentially data processing or communication."
Final Decision and Order by the Federal Communications Commission,
Docket No. 16979, March 10, 1971, Par. 27.

11. Digital computers (by far the majority of electronic
computers) are most efficiently served by a form of communication
(digital transmission) which was relatively rare before their
advent, and still is not common. Most electric communication circuits use the analog, not the digital, mode. But digital communication can be converted and deconverted to analog by circuit
attachments known as "modems" (modulator-demodulators).

12. At present, the different reliability criteria of computer systems for communication vs. those designed for data processing limit economies of integration. A communications utility
using presently available technology may find it unwise to use
the same computers routinely for data processing. However, over
the next decade the economies of integration are expected to increase, especially where communications systems are designed for
data rather than voice communications. D. D. Cowan and L. Waverman,
"The Interdependence of Communications and Data Processing: Issues
in Economies of Integration and Public Policy," Bell Journal of
Economics and Management Science 2, no. 2 (Autumn 1971): 657-77.

13. A compromise solution was reached for its Tele-center
Omni Processing System (TOPS) service, in which the brokerage
firms subscribing to the service themselves lease the access
lines and use them only for intrafirm messages in verifying and
executing buy and sell orders. Stuart M. Mathison and Philip M.
Walker, Computers and Telecommunications: Issues in Public Policy
(Englewood Cliffs, N. J.: Prentice-Hall, 1970), p. 52.

14. 4 FCC 155 (1937), cited ibid., p. 63. See also Final
Decision and Order, FCC Docket No. 16979, March 10, 1971, Par. 31.

15. Leonard Waverman, "Competition in Intercity Communications: Economies of Scale," paper read at the AT&T seminar,
Problems of Regulation and Public Utilities, 1971, Dartmouth College.

16. In the Matter of Use of the Carterfone Device in Message
Toll Telephone Service, Federal Communications Commission Dockets

Nos. 16942 and 17073. Order adopted June 26, 1968: 13 FCC 2d 420.

17. We lack evidence on pressures toward natural monopoly
in local microwave systems. Several firms newly entering communications at present have proposed local distribution by radio
carrier, variously suggesting the frequencies 11GHz, 18 GHz and
38.6-40 GHz for this purpose. Others advocate use of CATV (wired)
facilities for local distribution. See the submission by the
applicants in Federal Communication Commission Docket No. 18920.

18. See IBM Corporation Response in FCC Docket 16979, especially pp. 14-34 and 73 ff. According to IBM Fellow Dr. G. M. Amdahl,
the technology of 1966 (including System 360) would permit 100
to 200 terminals to use a single-purpose time-shared system; with
dissimilar and complex uses, the optimum number of users could drop
below 10. Again we must emphasize that these software problems
are not overcome by technological advances in hardware. They frequently grow worse.

19. Richard Posner in Computers, Communications, and the
Public Interest, ed. Martin Greenberger (Baltimore: Johns Hopkins
Press, 1971), pp. 243-44. Bell's previous attitude on this matter
indicates that for it, at least, the price might be a high one.
But it does not rule out interconnection: "When the Commission
determines that it is in the public interest to license additional
intercity common carriers, we would be willing to discuss with
them the technical arrangements required and appropriate charges
for any connections required of the telephone companies."--AT&T
submission quoted in First Report and Order, Federal Communications
Commission Docket No. 18920, May 25, 1971, Par. 152. In this Order
the Commission permitted DATRAN (Data Transmission Company) and
some other new firms to enter the field of communications as
common carriers.

20. Comments of American Telephone and Telegraph Company
before the Federal Communications Commission, Docket No. 18920,
October 1, 1970. The "Nationwide" rate structure imposes a discriminatory uniformity on various markets whose rates are the same
while costs are different. AT&T apparently intends to cut rates
in the lucrative markets to "meet" competition and to raise them
in the noncompetitive markets wherever the traffic will bear
an increase.

21. I assume here that the FCC will continue to regulate the
"competitive" services at least to the extent of applying minimum
cost criteria. If they were totally unregulated, they would probably fall under the ban of the Consent Decree of 1956 as far as
AT&T is concerned.

22. Alfred E. Kahn, The Economics of Regulation: Principles and Institutions (New York: John Wiley & Sons, 1970), 1: 83.

23. Ibid., pp. 83-85. A number of more minor objections are
suggested in footnotes.

24. Ibid., p. 75. Kahn notes that "the unit of production
(the single flight) which is the basis of cost incurrence, is
larger than the unit of sale (a single ticket to a single passen-
ger)." Hence the latter involves common costs attributable to the
former.

25. Ibid., p. 85n. This passage is immediately preceded by an admirably terse expression of the Tarif Vert principles of pricing (following Boiteux et al.): "If SRMC pricing did not cover ATC over time, capital would eventually be withdrawn and new capital, needed to meet a rising demand, repelled, until a recovering demand, moving up along a steeply rising MC curve, pushed prices up high enough and held them there long enough to attract new capital into the industry--with the possibility of a return of depressed prices with any temporary reemergence of excess capacity." Correct forecasting of long-run demand and the exact adjustment of capacity to this long-run demand is thus the key to correct pricing on a continuous basis of short-run marginal cost. (SRMC is short-run marginal cost, ATC average total cost, and MC marginal cost.)

26. Comments of AT&T, FCC Docket No. 18920, p. 59.

27. Ibid., p. 60.

28. It is a necessary but not sufficient element. Cf. Kahn, The Economics of Regulation, 2: 220-36. Even where natural mono- poly (long-run marginal cost less than average cost) is present, cream-skimming becomes a problem only when a discriminatory pricing structure in turn results from an institutional constraint on the utility firm requiring it to earn its permitted rate of return from intra-marginal rents.

29. Cf. William G. Shepherd, "The Competitive Margin in Communications," in Technological Change in Regulated Industries, ed. W. M. Capron (Washington, D.C.: Brookings Institution, 1971), pp. 111-12. "No serious observer has denied that the 'teamwork' arising from integration provides genuine advantages, but the Sys- tem has yet to offer any quantitative evidence about these bene- fits that could be compared with the possible costs. . . . The Bell System's tenacious defense, so devoid of data about these trade-offs, creates the suspicion that the principal usefulness of integration is in reinforcing exclusivity."

30. One may stipulate that no class of customers should pay rates higher than those that would be necessary for a supplier to serve it alone. Such rates can exist in a discriminatory pric- ing scheme, that is engineered to produce a certain overall rate of return, unless every other rate at least covers long-run mar- ginal cost including incremental profit requirements. They are likely to invite entry by rivals on a limited scale. When a rival offers to serve a single class of customers and can cover the resulting full average unit costs, including imputed externalities, with rates lower than the prevailing ones, it gives a clear signal that those rates are too high. This information may not be readily available in the absence of a challenge from the outside. But entry to a particular market may also be attempted by other sup- pliers, already established in other activities, whose marginal costs are lower than the regulated rates in the invaded market but higher than the marginal cost of the established supplier.

31. Final Decision and Order, FCC Docket No. 16979, March 10, 1971. The Commission required a "maximum separation of activities which are subject to regulation from non-regulated activities

involving data processing." This meant no commingling of activities and no use of computers in the common carriers' communications
systems for data processing.

32.   From the account in the Wall Street Journal, June 19,
1972. Eight applications to build domestic satellite systems were
on file at the FCC on the date of the decision, including one by
Microwave Communications, Inc. (MCI).

Index

Atlantic-Seaboard Formula: See Seaboard Formula
Averch-Johnson hypothesis: contrasted to Wellisz argument, 36;
    explained, 36; geometric exposition of, 36-37; limited by
    regulatory lag, 37; information requirements to implement,
    38; usefulness questioned, 47

Beta coefficients: as systematic risk, 54, 65, 76; for regulated
    industries, 65, 76; concept illustrated, 83
Boundary problem: in vertically integrated firms, 91; example in
    data communications, 91-94; as product of regulatory institu-
    tions, 107
Buchanan, James: economic theory of politics, 32

Cartels: stabilized by regulation, 32
Certification power: FPC use for social goals, xxiii-xxiv; FPC
    use in period of gas shortage, 46; and competitive entry, 95,
    97-99.
Coercion: defined, 3
Competition: contrasted to rivalry, 88
Competitive entry: example in data communications, 97-99; pro-
    spective results in data communications, 98
CRSP Investment Return File: relation to CRSP Master File, 60;
    described, 60-61
CRSP Master File: relation to CRSP Investment Return File, 60;
    described, 60-61

Data communications: example of boundary problem, 91-94; example
    of scale economies and integration, 95-97
Decision-making: process in general interdependence system, 4;
    government institutions, 6; as function of power, 7
Downs, Anthony: theory of political action, 29, 32

Economic paradigm: and the public utility institution, 2
Economies of scale: example in data communications, 95-97
Efficient resource allocation: as regulatory goal, xix, xxi, xxiv,
    85, 86; in gas shortage, 43; and marginal cost pricing, 46;

127

performance tests for, 86-87. See also Welfare economics
Entry restriction: in communications satellites, 104; and the
    boundary problem, 105; and economic efficiency, 105
Environmental quality: criterion for regulation, xxiii
Equity: as goal of regulation, 85, 86; criteria for, 87 See
    also Income redistribution

Government institutions: and economic power, 5, 6; as neutral
    power vehicle, 6; as decision-making device, 6
"Grass is always greener" fallacy: economist's misconception of
    regulation, 27, 88

Income redistribution: regulatory goal, xix, xxii; tax and expen-
    diture policy, xxi; unintended effect of regulation, xxiv;
    and government activity, 5; regulation as system of taxation,
    12; analysis of regulation in, 17; See also Equity
Industry structure: effect on regulatory control, 14
Institutions: and the allocation of power, 4, 31; origins of, 31;
    theory of, 31, 32

Judicialization of regulation: causes of, 17

Law: as power instrument, 5; and economic relations, 5
Legal paradigm: and the public utility institution, 2

Marginal cost: contrasted with fully allocated costs, 91; long-
    run, in data communications, 102-4
Marginal cost pricing: in rate structure, xxi; effects of, xxii;
    failure of regulation to achieve, 28; in gas shortage, 41, 42-
    43; effect on gas storage, 42; and efficient resource alloca-
    tion, 46; and telecommunications rates, 50, 99; and cross
    subsidization, 99; as a static economic concept, 99-100;
    difficulties of applying, 99, 100-102; in real time mode,
    100-101
Miller and Modigliani: perpetual growth case, 55-56, 79
Monopoly profits: restriction of, xix, xx, xxiv

Normative economics: usefulness of, 30

Olson, Mancur: theory of political action, 29
Opportunity set: defined, 3
Organization: costs of, 29

Pareto optimality: and the "grass is always greener" fallacy,
    27-28; theory of institutions, 31. See also Welfare Economics.
Political economy: approach to regulation, xxiv
Populist: spirit of regulation, xix
Power: defined, 3; as ability to manipulate, 7; implications of
    possession, 7; as means of increasing opportunity set, 13;
    as a check on power, 19-20; as instrument, 22; distribution
    and exercise, 29; dynamics of acquisition, 30
Power paradigm: and the public utility institution, 1, 23; as

morally neutral, 2; making operational, 24-25; as nonnormative, 25; connection with legal paradigm, 27; tautological character, 27

Progress: as a goal of regulation, 85, 86; standards for, 87

Property rights: as result of regulation, 12

Public utility institution: and the power paradigm, 1, 23; as power institution, 8, 9; participants in, 10; in conflict resolution, 24; as a result of power, 28

Rate-base: explained, 35; role in Averch-Johnson hypothesis, 37

Rate design: See rate structure

Rate of return: FPC use in gas shortage, 46; market equilibration of, 51, 58; associated with beta coefficient, 81

Rate of return regulation: explained, 35

Rate structure: effect on resource allocation, xxi; in data communications, 98-99

Reasonable regulator: defined, 55

Regulated firms: industries identified, 59

Regulation: and social problems, xxiii, xxiv; determines opportunity set, 9; and delegation of power, 10; and locus of power, 10; place in larger context of economic policy, 11; as means of organizing goals, 11; effectiveness, 11, 12, 106, 106-7; as property rights, 12; controlled by the regulated, 13-21, 26-27, 106; regulatee-oriented functions, 14-15; creates certainty and security, 15; provides sinecures for politicians, 15; goals of regulators, 16-17; goals of non-regulatees, 17; redistribution of income in, 17; uses to which put, 18-19; psychological aspects, 20-21; knowledge aspects, 21-22; results determined by power, 29; in interest of industry, 30; "reasonable" contrasted to "unreasonable," 54, 55, 56, 80; goals of 85; failure to deal with rivalry, 89; and competitive entry, 95; and alternative criteria, 102; and efficient resource allocation, 106

Results of regulation: versus structure, 22

Risks: regulated versus unregulated firms, 51; associated with returns, 76, 80-83

Rivalry: contrasted to competition, 88

Seaboard Formula: explained, 40; discourages storage, 40; and overcapacity, 40; effect on gas shortage, 41; compared with marginal cost pricing, 43; origins, 48

Stability: as goal of regulation, 85, 86

Stability in regulation: implications of, 87

Structure of regulation: versus results, 22

Telecommunications pricing policy: appropriate rate structure, 48-49, 99-103

Tullock, Gordon: economic theory of politics, 32

Unreasonable regulator: defined, 55

Vertical integration: between utility and manufacturing

affiliate, 89; through common facilities, 90; and nonregulated activities, 90-91. See also Boundary problem

Welfare economics: criterion for regulation, xx, xxi; place in regulation, xxi. See also Pareto optimality, Efficient resource allocation
Wellisz overcapacity thesis: contrasted to Averch-Johnson, 36; presented in pipeline case, 39-40
Working rules: defined, 3

Zajac, E. E.: geometric exposition of Averch-Johnson, 36-37